Somewhere, Nowhere

Somewhere, Nowhere

Ben Mallalieu

HOPCYN PRESS

Somewhere, Nowhere

© Ben Mallalieu 2015

First published in Great Britain in 2015 by Hopcyn Press Ltd.
www.hopcynpress.com

The right by Ben Mallalieu to be identified as the Author of the Work has been asserted by him in accordance with the Copyright, Designs and Patents Act 1988.

ISBN: 978-0-9928933-0-9

Printed and bound by Berforts Information Press.

'"It's a poor sort of memory that only works backwards,"
the Queen remarked.'
Lewis Carroll, *Alice through the Looking Glass*

Chapter 1

2007, 1974

I always regretted not going to Matala.

One snowy night in the early 1970s I was sleeping on a park bench in Munich when the police woke me up: 'If you cannot afford a hotel, you should go home,' they said in that sensible (if sinister) Germanic way; but it wasn't a decade for being sensible so I walked aimlessly around the city for a couple of hours trying and failing to find a place where I could sleep undisturbed. Eventually I gave up looking and spent the rest of the night shivering on the steps of a locked railway station while a bearded hippie told stories about a miraculous beach in Crete where the sun shone all winter and you could sleep in caves and live for next to nothing.

Unfortunately, I was already set on heading east to places with enticing but ultimately disappointing names like Menali and Mazar-al-Sharif, and by the time I got home Matala's best days were officially over. All that remained was Joni Mitchell's catchy, gently optimistic song, Carey, which celebrated drinking wine at the Mermaid café, getting beach tar on your feet and listening to scratchy rock and roll beneath a Matala moon, a eulogy for all the lost carefree times. Whenever I heard it, particularly in later decades, I wished I had gone to Matala. I never wanted to go back to Menali.

Matala was the first famous hippie beach and many respectable people became seriously upset – 'Worthless, sponging idlers,' said the otherwise sensible travel writer Ernle Bradford – although now it is hard to understand why. 'Bohemians' behaving badly had been a feature of many European beaches throughout the twentieth century and probably earlier, but this was for some reason different, something new and worse. Perhaps it was because hippies did not seem to care about money (perhaps rich idlers would have been more acceptable), or maybe it was the drugs: even the better Greek governments have never approved of cannabis – too Turkish (Turkish governments don't approve of it either, for much the same reason) – and those were especially mad days under the Colonels.

By most accounts, the hippies and the Matala locals coexisted reasonably happily; young Greeks were impressed, particularly the reluctant national servicemen stationed in southern Crete who thought it a far better lifestyle than fighting for colonel and country, but the Mermaid Cafe failed to survive the seventies. The owner had built an extension to his kitchen without the correct permission – hardly a serious offence, particularly in Greece – but he was locked up and tortured, and his cafe was closed. The caves were fenced off with barbed wire and the party was over. They paved the streets, built a car park and Matala quickly became popular with package tours.

When I finally got there thirty years late for the party, I wasn't hitch-hiking any more, nor sleeping on park benches; and our hotel room had clean white linen.

In Joni Mitchell's time, Matala amounted to a few small single-storey houses, none particularly beautiful, two beach cafes and a grocery shop. Now, it has a few hundred buildings, none bigger than three storeys, nor particularly ugly, although you would have to look hard to find any that are not rental apartments, gift shops, travel agents or tavernas. Most of the bigger package-tour hotels are further up the narrow valley, out of sight from the seafront, which helps maintain the illusion that little has changed.

The famous old graffiti on the sea wall – 'Welcome to Matala, George. Today is life. Tomorrow never comes' – has been repainted with more flowery, more emphatically sixtyish lettering. You can buy 'Today is life' T-shirts. But despite the package tour commercialism, Matala has retained a slightly raffish hippie air. A few recidivist old wrecks may even have been there ever since the sixties – a bit like going to a pub at opening time and finding the back room full of drunks locked in from the night before and hoping no one will notice. You also see younger, fashion-statement Euro-hippies with blond dreadlocks, and American babyboomers looking for the misspent youth they might have had if they hadn't accepted the graduate traineeship at General Motors or IBM; but most people are typical tourists, although not many are English and even fewer are Greek.

The side of the bay with the caves has been left undeveloped with a small grove of dusty evergreen trees I couldn't identify next to the beach. I asked at the taverna what they are called: 'They are just trees,' the waiter said confidently. 'They don't have a name.'

The town is not at its best in the afternoon when the beach fills up with coachloads of nouveau bourgeois Russians on day excursions from the bigger resorts along the coast. They are interested in the hippies – an episode in recent history they missed out on – and I overheard a group asking the deckchair man what the village was like then, but he didn't know: he wasn't there either.

But, just up the coast, the once-famous Red Beach has changed very little, protected from development because it can only be reached by a twenty-five minute scramble over the headland, a bit of a slog on the first day but easy by the end of the week. The cliffs are the colour of rock candy, the earth covered in fine white dust; the light is blinding, the silence almost deafening and there are moments on the walk when you can imagine (pretend) that not much has changed since Minoan times.

Sometime in the recent past, a Belgian sculptor has carved animals and ancient Egyptian symbols into the rocks. The sand is large-grained and soft to walk on with outcrops of black granite smoothed and sculpted by the sea. The water is safe, protected by cliffs on either side, and warm enough for swimming long after autumn has come and gone in England.

In the evening when the crowds had left, my wife Jenny and I sat outside the Lions taverna on the Matala seafront drinking Cretan wine and watching the last of the sunlight on the caves. Sunsets don't change much; the night was still full of stars and the old rock and roll drifting across the water from the other bars – Bob Dylan's 119th Dream, Shine

On You Crazy Diamond, lots of Bob Marley – was up to scratch.

From a distance, the caves look like a natural phenomenon but, close to, you can see that they are man made, even older than Petra, carved into the honeycombed stone in early classical times and still full of echoes of former occupants, although few of them particularly fashionable: the Roman used the caves as catacombs; lepers lived there in the days before beautiful beaches were an asset to be exploited and ruined. The heat of the sun sinks deep into the rock keeping it warm at night and possibly all winter. I could see myself in the 1970s living in a cave with a cheesecloth curtain over the doorway and a sleeping bag on the stone bed, and I wouldn't have needed much else in those days. But you can't sleep there any more.

In the Lions Taverna, the paper tablecloth was decorated with a map of Crete with, just below it, a tiny triangular island almost obscured by the metal clip holding the cloth to the table. 'Didn't St Paul go there?' I asked as its name rang the faintest of bells, a faded Post-it note at the back of the brain.

'Oh yes,' said the manager confidently. 'That was where he was shipwrecked, he and the ninety-nine saints,' but I didn't believe him as I was pretty certain that Paul had only been shipwrecked once and that was on Malta, and I would have remembered the ninety-nine saints if the Acts of the Apostles had mentioned them – saints rarely come in batches of ninety-nine.

I asked what the island was like now and the manager pulled a face as though fearing he was about to lose another customer. 'It's like Matala was forty years ago,' he said sadly.

Chapter 2

2008

Today is Saturday; I need to write that down because my phone is dead and my watch has stopped, perhaps appropriate on an island where time and the outside world make little impression – nowhere else have I had so little sense of 'I should be somewhere else' or 'I should be doing something more' – but mighty inconvenient when I have a ferry and plane to catch a week on Friday. I can roughly tell the time of day from the shadow of a stick in the sand, but there is no easy way of telling the day of the week other than by keeping a record.

This morning, there are no new human footprints on my part of the beach, but a cat has added my tent to its silent nightly round.

A naked old man with an impossibly long white beard dances along the shoreline, greeting the sunrise. He looks like the 'It's…' man from Monty Python and he moves with improbable fluency for someone of his age. He can sing well too, mostly snatches from old Beatles songs. His name is Wolfgang and his philosophy of life is simple: 'Everything is easy,' he says.

If you are eating, he has the initially disconcerting habit of helping himself uninvited to your food, but after a few days you cease to notice. I have some raggle-taggle friends who live in the woods – Louis and Kristina, Panos and Nadia, the Hungarian baker whose name I always forget, others who come and go – and I cannot walk past their camp without being offered tea or beer or food, which is almost embarrassing until I realise that this is how life ought to be.

The island is sometimes said to be Ogygia where the goddess Calypso kept Odysseus prisoner for seven years, although the supporting evidence is tenuous: in terms of flora, fauna and geography, it fails to tick almost any of the right boxes, but then neither do any of the other possible claimants. Ogygia is surely as mythological as the Celtic island of Tír na nÓg (is the similarity of names just a coincidence?) where the hero Oisín discovered to his cost that for every day he spent there a year had gone by at home (he didn't have a working watch, either). But I am happy to think of this island as Ogygia because it is, perhaps more that any place I have ever been to, enchanted.

And it is certainly difficult to escape from: ferry connections are unreliable and you can be marooned here for days, sometimes weeks, if the wind is blowing in the wrong direction.

The permanent indigenous population is said to be around thirty-five with a similar number of semi-permanent 'outsiders' from the rest of Greece and Europe. I have been told several times that there are people living on the island whom nobody ever sees, but I am not certain what they mean; perhaps something horrific, or at any rate slightly odd, is going on just out of sight. It has no hotels and fewer than a hundred apartment beds for tourists; most summer migrants sleep on the beaches or under the trees, which is how it was on most Greek islands forty years ago but is now usually frowned upon, not to say actively discouraged by the police.

The island is inevitably changing, but fortunately only slowly. The road has been paved in the last year or so, the harbour at Karave enlarged; there might even be proper electricity soon [but probably not]. A few new houses are being built – although I see no evidence of anyone working on them – on the road to Agios Ioannis, but the road stops at Sophia's taverna, from where it is a half-mile walk over the rocks, through the woods and far away from the twenty-first century to the beach where I am living under a juniper tree.

Pines and tamarisks are fine and good in their different ways, and palm trees, nodding or otherwise, are a welcome feature on half the world's best beaches, but the sea juniper, the Greek cedar, *juniperus oxycedrus macrocarpa*, is the best of all beach trees, and this tiny island is home to what is probably the largest sea juniper forest anywhere in the world.

No other trees, not even yews and olives, look so old, with twisted limbs bleached like bone. It is as though they have suddenly frozen in the middle of some extravagant activity to which they will return as soon as your back is turned, a game of grandmother's footsteps.

The ancient Egyptians used juniper oil for embalming their dead. Current opinion insists that this was distilled from juniper wood rather than from the berries although I have read that sea juniper berries, almost certainly from the island, were found in the tomb of Tutankhamen, with no obvious explanation of their use.

During their flight into Egypt, Joseph and Mary hid Jesus from Herod's soldiers under a juniper tree; from earliest times, its berries were seen as a protection against witches and serpents, its smoke used to purify temples and ward off plague. In classical and medieval Europe and in pre-Columbian America it was widely used as a contraceptive – Pliny the Elder recommends rubbing the penis with crushed juniper berries before intercourse, and, if that didn't work as it probably didn't, as a means of inducing miscarriage. In the seventeenth and eighteenth centuries juniper oil became a popular if ineffective cure for the clap and, more lastingly, as a flavouring for gin – perhaps gin's reputation as an abortion agent owes more to the juniper than the alcohol (it can often be found in the list of ingredients for Victorian patent remedies, particularly those like Beecham's Pills that were advertised as suitable for 'women's ailments').

The berries used as a spice are mostly *juniperus communis*, the common juniper of more northern latitudes, or in classical times from *juniper excelsa* or *phoenicia* of which there are many on the island, mostly inland, a good tree as Mediterranean conifers go, but less magical.

In the nineteenth century in the Appalachian mountains in particular juniper was the timber of choice for makers of moonshine whisky – it burnt without smoke and didn't alert the revenue officers. Its timber is still widely used for clothes cupboards, its oil acting as a deterrent to moths.

But no one collects juniper berries or anything else from the island any more, not for any purpose.

The beach is flat for the first thirty or forty yards from the sea then then rises increasingly steeply into the dunes, with the first line of trees about sixty yards from the shore; my hammock hangs from the wide-spreading branches of one of them. The tree leans forward towards the sea, giving welcome shade from the midday sun; it is fifteen feet high and forty across, a largely chaotic tangle of branches, dusty and ancient, silver grey – the colour of burnt foil from a cigarette packet – and astringent to the touch like the taste of quinine. Some branches have grown horizontally for centuries and then for no obvious reason changed their minds. The tree's life history makes no sense unless its perception of up and down has changed dramatically on several occasions (much like most life histories, particularly mine). Like a banyan, juniper branches can put down roots and its roots can sprout new trunks. Perhaps most of the trees in the wood share, or once shared, a common root system like British elm trees, before they all died, or a giant fairy ring.

The main trunk bends back on itself like a meandering river; part of it, more dormant than most, stretches horizontally out to sea like a hand with grasping fingers, the hand of glory (open the gates and the hand of glory shall come in), a kraken emerging tentatively from its monstrous shell.

Twenty years or more ago, a previous occupant sawed through a few of the lower branches to improve the living space – it wouldn't be allowed now; the hippies are very protective of their forest; even the dead wood is left alone although for centuries it was pollarded and coppiced without ill effect.

In front of the tree, the sand is buttressed by a rough dry-stone wall to create a flat terrace for pitching a tent. It is a good place to live.

Half way between my camp and the sea, the skeleton of an old tree is almost certainly dead although you can never be entirely sure: it still retains a kind of potential energy, much like an electricity pylon or the site of an old battlefield (if that makes any sense). It has the astonished look of a sleeper who dreams he has been turned into a dead tree then wakes to find that it wasn't a dream. A useful rule with wood on the island is that if you can't pick it up it is probably alive.

Dead juniper wood takes centuries to decay in the dry air, immaculately preserved like the bodies of medieval saints; sometimes you can identify the site of old houses just from the roof timbers while the stone walls are scattered or overgrown and no longer immediately obvious. (According to Pliny the original juniper beams of the temple of Diana in Saganum, built 'two hundred years before the conquest of Troy', were still in perfect condition.)

Mosquito nets and hammocks hang like cobwebs and moths' nests between the branches of many of the trees, decorated with flotsam and jetsam like Derek Jarman's garden at Dungeness, treading the thin line between art and litter. Rows of pots and pans top the makeshift stone-and-pebble walls but the people have blended into the landscape to become almost invisible, their lean bodies the colour of the sand. Close to, they look like ancient Greeks but with longer dreadlocks and a disconcerting 'eighteen going on eight hundred' look, prematurely aged by the sun and wind but kept permanently young by the simple life, living close to nature if not to what most people would call reality. In Homeric times, to have glittering eyes was a sign of a god in human form; now it is a sign of a misspent youth.

At midday, I sit outside Sophia's taverna in the shade and catch the breeze which blows a siren-like note across the top of my beer bottle. Sophia's is one of the new buildings but it sells proper old-fashioned Cretan food, a choice of only two hot dishes – meat or vegetable – baked in the oven in the morning and kept warm on a hot plate until evening.

Pieter the Painter, one of the taverna locals, used to be a software designer in Holland, painting in his spare time and occasionally spending his holidays on the island. Six years ago, he painted a portrait of a taverna owner who liked it so much he gave him a house, saying: 'Every island should have a painter.' He has been here ever since, at first painting taverna signs for a living, later establishing an international reputation as an artist with exhibitions in Athens, Amsterdam and Vienna. He is building a geodesic 'egg', the Kalletechneion, which will be the island's arts centre with its facilities open to anyone who wants to use them.

The island also has a small group of Russian philosophers doing whatever it is that Russian philosophers do, and possibly a journalist: a copy of the island's newspaper is dated 'Sometime in November'; the front, and only, page is covered with doodles and at the bottom is written 'Sorry, there is no news today'. [When I go home to my office in Farringdon Road, London, I sincerely wish all newspapers could be like that.]

The island has no banks, no cash tills, no one who accepts credit cards or travellers cheques, no post box, no pavements, no parking lots. No income tax officials, no forms to fill in. No builders, no estimates, no bank statements, no news of the affairs of men. No one sells T-shirts emblazoned with the island's name. The capital, Kastri, does not have a single shop. It used to have a beekeeper, quietly spoken and liked by all, but one morning a whole ferryload of troops and armed police landed unscheduled in a hurry and took him away.

Today is Monday.

Anna is Greek with a Minoan kind of beauty; she studies modern dance in Paris and spends her summers on the island with a little dog with large ears (a bat with four legs). Walking round the headland to Lavrakas beach, I find her standing alone nearly up to her waist in the sea, bending forward and dipping her hair in the water then slowly swinging her head and body round to make catherine wheels of water in the air. It could be a scene from a Knossos fresco.

Later, I meet her on a sand dune to watch the sunset. We drink ginger tea and someone (Greek with long hair and beard, not immediately distinguishable from many other Greeks on the island with long hair and beards) plays a musical instrument with a series of metal blades like a jew's harp attached to a wooden sound box, twanging the keys and drumming with his fingers. The island is full of noises; sounds and sweet airs. We sit in a row like Easter Island statues.

This is the most southerly of all the Greek islands, closer to Africa than Athens, once a half-way house between Ancient Egypt and Pre-classical Greece, and if you look closely you can still see traces of both, almost as alive as ever (or so it sometimes seems). At night there is no light pollution; the sky is as heavy with stars as the Blake engraving from the Book of Job, I Am Young and Ye Are Very Old. (Possibly the other way round; perhaps when engraved and printed it became a mirror image: every virgin was a harlot once.)

In the starlight, Anna dances a slow duet with her favourite tree.

Today is Tuesday.

Lili and Sara, Spanish exchange students at the University of Herakleion, are living under the next-door tree; they remind me of two friends I briefly knew when travelling thirty years ago. In the morning, the three of us go for a walk led by a gentle young Greek (with long black hair and beard). We would never have found the path without him, a hard climb under a hot sun and a six hundred feet scramble down the side of a ravine. Journey's end is Potamos, surely one of the most beautiful beaches in the world, with half a mile of the best golden sand gently shelving into safe, clear water, with an amphitheatre of cliffs. Apart from us, it is entirely deserted.

After one of the best and most refreshing swims of my life, I hang my hammock beneath the branches of a sea juniper and fall asleep listening to the waves, the cicadas, the bees in the thyme, the occasional bleat and tonk of a goat and Lili and Sara laughing in the sea.

Today is now. Tomorrow never comes.

Chapter 3

2008

The sea between here and Crete is much deeper than it ought to be, twice as deep as the White Mountains are high, or so it's said; and, just around the corner to the south is the last Mediterranean refuge of fin and sperm whales and possibly much else. Jonah would have met his fish near here. St Paul nearly did the same, and Guy Crouchback in Evelyn Waugh's Officers and Gentlemen had an equally troubled journey in 1941 escaping the fall of Crete; one night, half delirious, he woke to find the drifting boat surrounded by shining humps and the sea singing with a low resonant note. 'Was it real?' he later thought. Another night, he saw 'the calm plain fill with myriads of cats' eyes', In the light of his torch, 'the whole surface of the water was encrusted with carapaces gently bobbing one against the other and numberless ageless lizard-faces gaping at him as far as his light reached.'

From where I lie in my hammock under the tree, the White Mountains are sometimes clearly visible on the horizon; often they disappear in the mist; other times it is hard to decide what is mountain and what is cloud. (First there is a mountain, then there is no mountain, then there is.)

I can usually see the route of St Paul's journey – he was travelling in October, too late in the season, and after leaving the Fair Havens in Crete, just along the coast on the far side east of Matala, his ship was hit by an easterly storm, the Euroclydon, notorious in this stretch of water in times past. Trying and failing to make a safe landing at each of the beaches in turn, they had to take what shelter they could round the corner to the west under the lee of the cliffs, where only with great difficulty were the sailors able to bail out the boat and bind the hull with cables to stop it breaking apart; but the storm lasted another fourteen days while 'neither sun nor stars could be seen' before the ship gave up the ghost off the coast of Malta. Not a good journey.

Did the the captain's bravado deflate into panic and then despair, or did he keep a brave front throughout? The Bible doesn't say which, interested only in the acts of apostles themselves. Byron's Don Juan was hit by a westerly storm (his path, Odysseus's and St Paul's may have crossed although many centuries and reality dimensions apart); the captain of his ship also had to bind the hull with sail and rope, but to less effect – the poem has a good description of a panicking crew and, like Officers and Gentlemen, of being adrift in an open boat, but he has little to say about the pirate's island – somewhere in Greece – where he is washed up. I had hoped it might have been mine but there is no evidence one way or another. Where was Gilbert's Little Billee shipwrecked?

An American friend, Bob Gaesser, with whom I spent a few happy days in Peshawar and Kabul, was once shipwrecked in the Straits of Malacca. All the lifeboats were chained up and the padlocks painted over and impenetrable; the crew ran about the deck screaming but Bob and the friend he was travelling with were both far too stoned and just sat there laughing. That was probably not the case with St Paul.

One morning I hear the call of of something lost behind the hills (for lust of knowing what should not be known), and I set off intending to head south-east but the contours of the island usually insist on a much more roundabout itinerary. The bottom of the ravines are green with dense scrub, mostly stunted pine and arbutus between sandstone boulders; further inland, the trees grow twenty feet high with a spread of fifty, and more heather and less thyme than on the coast. The higher valleys are steep sided, their floors a carpet of dust and pine needles.

I walk for half a day, although never in a straight line and rarely in the right direction, scrambling over the top of the island without seeing another person and rarely crossing a path, with only an occasional startled partridge for company. Sometimes, walls indicate where fifty years ago had been fields, before the island's population dwindled from five hundred to fewer than fifty, but now it is almost all pine forest. (One day, most of it will all go up in flames: all it needs is sunlight refracting through a broken bottle – *igne natura renovatur integra*, by fire nature is renewed whole; that is perhaps the way of things.)

And then on the far side, high on the edge of the cliffs on the hypotenuse of the island, I find a small group of houses unlike anything else, and I know I have arrived somewhere special. I was told that a group of Russian 'philosophers' live somewhere nearby – former space scientists or nuclear physicists or something of that kind, and this is them – but even when forewarned the reality comes as a bit of a shock: this isn't the kind of place you expect to find on a Greek island, or anywhere else. (Something is happening but you don't know what it is.)

The first comparison that comes to mind is with The Magus when the 'hero' walks through the pine forests of Spetses to be confronted with the sinister world beyond the 'Waiting Room' where nothing is quite as it seems and will never be quite the same again. (This is a very free exposition of the plot.)

John Fowles wrote eloquently about the strangeness of Greek islands, and this island certainly has its weird moments, which is one of the reasons why I like it (although other people might not feel the same). But this isn't at all weird: it quickly seems to be the most natural thing in the world for a group of Russian scientists to build a surreal community on the southernmost tip of Europe and be waiting for me to turn up.

It reminds me mostly of the remote Central Asian monastery of the Sarmoung Brotherhood which the esoteric philosopher Gurdjieff claimed to have visited in Meetings With Remarkable Men. But the Russians aren't part of a cult, just a small group of hospitable, intelligent people who happen to like living in one of the more beautiful places in the world: the cliffs here are higher and steeper than on Santorini – above the clouds on bad days – and they face due west to an unbroken horizon, an uninterrupted sunset. It shouldn't be thought unusual to find a group of middle-aged Russians belatedly enjoying the free-thinking youth they'd been denied by the Brezhnev regime, a peace dividend after half a lifetime at the coal face of the Cold War in Space City or Chernobyl.

They are happy to invite me for supper and show me round. A circular building has a pyramid roof made of green wine bottles and windows of car windscreens, the stones in the walls fitting together as neatly as in an Inca monument. A small house has been cut into the rock with a glass wall looking out to sea; this is 'the writer's room', currently empty. I am shown a book by the last person to live there – five-hundred pages without capital letters or punctuation. Another two rooms are entirely subterranean, accessed through a small trapdoor: one is a hexagon, the other a pentagon with a floor pattern based on a design by MC Escher. Electricity comes from solar panels and a multicoloured wind generator made of recycled washing machine drums. A beam of light shines vertically into the night sky as a marker for any UFOs that might be passing, and they are building a funicular railway a thousand foot down to the sea. I tell them about the funicular railway between Linton and Linmouth powered by water from the river. 'We will power our one with beer,' says Igor.

The Russians grow their own food, paint pictures, make beautiful things (sensible and absurd), do nobody any harm and spend their spare time considering Pythagorean philosophy and the practical possibilities of immortality, all in all not a bad life.

And Gurdjieff turns out to be their favourite philosopher, which is particularly surprising as he is hardly a fashionable thinker – too deep for most people, too much like hard work for me. I enjoyed Meetings With Remarkable Men, but I couldn't say I was any the wiser by the end of it, a series of misleading tales that take the reader on a wild goose chase where nothing can be believed at face value. I never attempted Beelzebub's Tales to His Grandson which brings the concept of a 'difficult' book into a different dimension, but perhaps uniquely among modern philosopher-mystics Gurdjieff was capable of laughing at himself, and there is plenty of laughter when dining with the Russians.

It is like somewhere I have always been destined to go to without realising it, or maybe somewhere I have been to many times already only to forget all about it the moment I leave.

Is it real?

Chapter 4

2009 perhaps

Someone is making breakfast on the embers of last night's fire and the damp smell of wood smoke hangs in narrow seams in the still salt air, intertwining slowly with the smell of pine resin and coffee. The co-mingling scent is as intoxicating as opium or frankincense, or so it seems as I lie half awake in my hammock, my outdoor cathedral, my million-star hotel. I trail my hand in the sand; floating, infinitely comfortable, a still point in a slowly turning world.

The sea glints through the trees. Nadia is kneeling by the fire, wearing someone else's shirt and jeans rolled up at the legs and sleeves; she hums a tune I cannot quite recognise (but nearly, just slightly out of reach; I know it in my sleep).

Last night, we cooked a large dish of chickpeas with onions and tomatoes, local olive oil and wild thyme from the woods. Other people brought wine and raki. The bottom of the pans are black with soot. Later, I will wash them in the sea, kneeling by the water's edge, scouring them with sand, one of the better daily rituals like collecting firewood (picking pine cones from the trees like ripe apples – it takes four to boil a kettle), and the twice weekly walk to Sarakiniko or the harbour to shop and drink a beer while recharging the laptop battery, the words I intend to write forming and reforming in my head as I walk along the coastal path, my footsteps changing with the rhythm of the sentences.

Nothing lasts. Not food. Nor people, perhaps. Books fall apart (the centre cannot hold). But the woods have always been here. The Egyptians came in quinqueremes (or was that someone else?) to gather juniper for embalming their dead, butting past my hammock, waking me with their sudden incomprehensible chatter and then when I look up they are gone. All good dreamers come this way some day. St Paul will have seen these woods as he sailed past, although his mind was probably on other things, driven by the storm. What would he have made of us, living without any concept of original sin?

We are living for nothing. Am I keeping some kind of a record, full of secrets to impart to the world when the time is right? No, this is it.

Kristina carries a chipped blue-and-white enamel mug very carefully as though it is unimaginably precious, a couple of inches of coffee at most inside, black and opaque with an elusive multicoloured film on top, like petrol on a wet road. She puts it on the rock beside my hammock. Echoes of other realities. There is sand in my sleeping bag, new mosquito bites on the back of my hand and above my right eyebrow, probably beach tar on my feet, but I don't care; a gust of cold sea air sends a shiver of happiness down my back.

I shall come, as most men think, to little good, but come to Oxford and my friends no more; tired of knocking on preferment's door, still crazy after all these years.

My hammock hangs between a pine tree (the rope cuts into the trunk causing the sap to run) and a sea juniper, on which it makes no impression: junipers grow as hard as box and just as slowly, their branches often dying back for years, standing out above the canopy like a crown of thorns, then for no obvious reason coming back to life, not dead but sleeping: was that why the Egyptians thought them so special? (According to Dr Ernest Parkin of Oxford University, 'the word's etymology is in the Latin "iuniperis", literally "youth-renewing" from "iuuenis" young, and "parere" to produce'.)

Last night, Panos sang all the Tom Waits songs he could remember (many), the fire casting a giant shadow of his dreadlocks against the tree canopy.

Where do we come from? Who are we? Where are we going? Do we care?

Soon the weather will change; without saying anything, people are starting to think about leaving. They already have that pensive look – 'Maybe I'll go to Thailand or maybe Venezuela…' They are still natural nomads; I used to be one too but my travelling days are over; I am not going anywhere: this really is my home: there is no retreat from here, no other shore. I have eaten too much of the goblin fruit, slept too long on the fairy hill. Unlike Odysseus, I will end my days in these green mansions, under the greenwood tree, in an anarchist state by the sea.

On the island, stars are not impossibly far away; here, the sky is in some almost tangible sense three dimensional. At night as we walk a while along the shore, the phosphorescent sea runs through our veins, we are clothed with the heavens and crowned with the stars. We dance beneath a diamond sky, to the end of love, by the light of the moon.

Igor told a long, complicated story, one that kept doubling back on itself, starting again from a different point, always threatening to head off at tangents with no clear indication of what was the main stream and what was an irrelevant backwater in danger of becoming an oxbow, a bit like the way Gurdjieff told stories. Its essence (or so it later appeared) was that the ancient Egyptians had been physically able to communicate with their dead ancestors who ordered their lives and told them which of their relatives to marry and have children with. But it all started to go wrong with the arrival of the Jewish slaves; the bloodlines became confused and the lines of communication were broken. This was why the Jews were expelled. He says that all Jewish theology stems from having once been party to a great truth that they cannot quite recapture. Or something like that. I wished I had been paying more attention.

Igor is Jewish and puzzled that my sister and my eldest daughter should both have Jewish godfathers, but far too polite to ask why.

In 1821, Shelley wrote to Mary Godwin: 'My greatest content would be utterly to desert all human society. I would retire with you and our child to a solitary island in the sea, would build a boat, and shut upon my retreat the floodgates of the world.'

But this is a way of life that will not survive; soon, people won't to be able to live like this. In the nineteenth century, Malcolm Arnold regretted the 'sick hurry and divided aims' of modern life; sixty years ago, Malcolm Lowry mourned the encroachment of 'civilisation', the 'creator of deathscapes, like a dull-witted fire of ugliness and ferocious stupidity', but there were always places – just a little more remote – where you could find sanctuary. Is this finally the end of the line, the last domino to fall?

'Whatever happened to Freedom?' said Panos as he stretches awake in his hammock. 'I use to go there often in the sixties. It was such a good place.'

They fucked it up; they always do. They didn't intend to; it was just the way it happened, the way it always happens. Once the word got out, more and more people wanted to go there, understandably because it was special, so they paved the road to make access easier and built an airport nearby so that people could come in their thousands for two weeks of Freedom. You can't blame them – fifty weeks of Slavery can't be fun – but the place changed, inevitably for the worse. Everything suddenly had its price and had to be rationed.

Then the police began deporting the undesirables – those people (like us) who thought Freedom was theirs by right all the time, not a luxury to be earned or a two-week escape. We no longer fitted in with the new smart image of the place as advertised in the brochures; we didn't look right, too real. Some of the harder cases complained and were put on 'Freedom substitute' which didn't do their heads any good but the authorities claimed the withdrawal symptoms would be easier to deal with.

Perhaps the woods will survive: in the woods lie madness, a freedom of a kind; during his frequent emotional breakdowns in Morte d'Arthur, Sir Lancelot ran off and became a wild man of the woods in places much like this. In the middle ages, the words 'wood' and 'mad' shared a common meaning, not surprisingly: both were the antithesis of the safe, tamed society and the well-tempered environment.

When people think they hear someone calling their name it is sometimes said to be a sign of madness, sometimes of religious enlightenment. In the middle ages, the two shared common ground.

Chapter 5

2009/2010

The scene vanishes as quickly as a fairy camp in Celtic mythology, or something half remembered, increasingly forgotten, like the Piper at the Gates of Dawn; Rip Van Winkle wakes to find his flintlock rusted away in the grass beside him; the faery gold turns to sand; then I awoke and behold it was all a dream, a 'secondary world' where disbelief has been only temporarily suspended. The memory of the smell of a dead woodfire remains, and with it an unavoidable if not entirely understandable sense of failure: the sailors gone under the sea, the dancers under the hill. A rude awakening.

Last year I stayed in England, weighed down by too many complications – everything is difficult – my health increasingly fragile, although I felt sure, without any real justification (or at least none that would be acceptable to any doctor), that it would improve as soon as I set foot on the island, my life an endless round of meetings with specialists who listened to the same story and asked the same questions but rarely came up with anything new; moving home, selling our house in London, trying and failing to buy somewhere smaller and cheaper in the country that suited everyone; further than ever from anywhere I wanted to be.

The island was almost out of sight. I briefly nursed hopes that we might all go and live there and it would be like My Family and Other Animals only better, but it is never going to happen.

Pieter the Painter has a friend called Clio, a postgraduate student at the Royal College of Art in London. She was on the island last summer but now she is lost in the big city knowing no one. We meet for a drink, exchange emails and never meet again. I know I am letting her down. I should be introducing her to places and people I know and seeing the familiar road through new eyes. Igor emails from the island to ask if I would like to join their community and then, when I don't reply, emails again in case that his first message went astray. And Sara from the beach is working in a Spanish restaurant in Manchester; she is coming to London soon: did I know of a good place to stay? I wish I could say: 'My home is your home; my life is your life', but I can't. (We have our broken dreams and do not think of them.) I know I am letting them down.

When we were selling the London house, strangers came up to me in the street to say they had heard I was moving and wished me well, which was a pleasant surprise although it undermined the anonymity I always hoped I'd been enjoying in London. There might be a whole world going on that I never notice; perhaps that's why I could never be any good as a novelist.

I saw all my possessions leave in a van and wondered with what might have seemed surprising nonchalance if I would ever see them again. My old man said follow the van. Farewell sorrow, praise God the open door, I ain't got no home in this world any more. And every place shall be my native home. All manner of places.

Chapter 6

2010/1949

It is a bright morning and we are absurdly early for the ferry so Jenny says: 'Why don't we stop off and see Liphook?' Once, we wouldn't have needed a detour, when the main road to the coast ran through the village, right between the house I used to live in and the Anchor, one of the old Hampshire coaching inns, but it was bypassed long ago, becoming an oxbow of road, and Liphook is just a name I see on a motorway signpost; I often mention it when we drive past but usually there is no time to make the detour.

Deja vu may work like the beginning of an oxbow; the brain's perception of time does not always proceed on a straight track, sometimes unconsciously meandering and occasionally it begins to break through where the bend doubles back on itself so that the same sensory input is experienced twice, the first time as an 'echo' in advance; the mind rarely works along purely linear lines.

I lived in the house for the first two and a half years of my life and I remember nothing about it – I have even forgotten its name – but I would once have known my way around; I could have walked from one end of the garden to the other and from the front door to my bedroom as though I owned the place; but I don't remember anything. The memory is entirely buried.

It is a bright morning and I am listening to Harry Nilsson's Aerial Pandemonium Ballet for the first time in thirty years, an album almost entirely forgotten, perhaps unfairly – I remembered having liked it, the summer before I left for India, and said so to my daughter who downloaded it from the internet and gave it to me as a birthday present, and I am amazed how easily it all comes back. I have no idea which track is coming next but when the music starts I can suddenly recall the words of the first line and then at the end of the first line I can suddenly remember the second... 'And in 1941, a happy father has a son...'

For a long time, we cannot find anywhere to park, which is odd and, considering my past – admittedly long past – connections with the place, slightly unsettling, muddying the deeper waters of memory, disturbing the monsters sleeping in the silt. A car park attached to some kind of secretive government office has plenty of empty spaces, but, when we pull in, it feels as though net curtains are being twitched in all the neighbouring buildings, and even though it is nine o'clock on a Saturday morning we both independently conclude that we ought to look elsewhere. The Anchor has a chain across the entrance to its car park (there is a certain logic to this, if tortuous – and inconvenient – a symbolic truth of no practical value), but eventually we find a single empty space on the road out of the village right next to the wall of what used to be my garden, the kind of high stone wall with old roses spilling over, the kind usually found in illustrations to Beauty and the Beast, the kind of wall I've wanted all my life. As a baby, not that I remember it, my pram was often parked on the other side under the elm trees (also long gone) at the end of the garden where the rooks nested; I learnt to caw before I could talk, or so it was said.

The music doesn't stop when Jenny switches off the ignition and we climb out of the car... 'and in 1944 the father walks right out the door...' Much though I like it, fondly as I remember it, it has the persistence and inevitability of a falling line of dominoes, like someone else's cat that keeps jumping up on your lap and at first you think 'how friendly' but soon you give serious thought to giving it a punch when its owner isn't looking. 'And in 1961...' Why has no one thought of using it in a television ad? It sticks in the mind like chewing gum on the sole of your shoe on a hot day.

The house I used to live in has become a branch of Lloyds Bank; inside, it looks like any other bank – they all look alike really, all peculiarly soulless – and it is hard to imagine that it was ever anyone's home, least of all mine, or that some of the furniture in my London house might once have stood in this actual room where people are queuing up to pay in cheques or take out money or help themselves, or not, to their stupid leaflets. I cannot recognise anything.

The garden is now home to more than a hundred houses, none of which I could afford to buy even if I wanted to, which I don't.

Liphook is a ghastly place. (Why had I never noticed the awfulness of the name?) What on earth possessed my parents to buy it? Presumably it was the usual kind of compromise that ends up satisfying nobody. The village is claustrophobic middle England, a time capsule where life itself has been bypassed, lived, if at all, at one step removed, in suspended animation, an oxbow of stagnant water.

The newsagent stocks a limited but predictable selection of newspapers; all with feature articles offering insights into the lives of 'celebrities' whom the inhabitants of Liphook will never meet but would dearly love to resemble in any way they can (so long as it doesn't involve taking risks or breaking ranks), even down to the stupidest details; their comment pages are full of hysterical warnings of barbarians at the gates – Gypsies, benefit scroungers, squatters, anarchists, illegal immigrants, asylum seekers and the like, none of whom are ever likely to set foot in their safe enclave (which somehow only makes them appear more frightening). Years ago when my parents ate dinner in the Anchor, people at other tables would make rude remarks about 'socialists' in loud pointed voices. (My father was then a Labour member of parliament and the Labour government of 1945 was not popular in middle England, possibly more unpopular in middle England than any government before or since.) It is hard to imagine either the food or the company has improved much. Probably worse.

The only new friends my parents made or talked about later were a family called the Conrans who had seen better times. (Their business importing spices had been an early casualty of the war, or maybe I am confusing them with some other family my parents knew.) Their teenage son Terry failed all his exams except art, an added worry for his parents but not unexpected; when partnering my mother at darts in the public bar of the Anchor she had to add up the scores because he could never get it right, but it didn't hold him back in later life.

My mother bought a stuffed sailfish in a glass case at a local auction. Friends laughed when they saw it so she gave it to the fishmonger down the road who hung it in pride of place on the back wall behind the counter. I rather hope we might find it still there, but there is no sailfish and no fishmonger's any more. Once, as I was later told, all the family put our palm prints in a square of wet cement beside the front door of our house – mine must have been very small – but they aren't there either.

Chapter 7

2010

We are staying, between houses, with an old friend who has a beautiful garden. It is one of my favourite places in England, a temporary refuge, an unexpected oasis, a 'clearing' in a wood surrounded by open, windswept and rainswept fields close to the cliffs (increasingly close), an unlikely place to find a beautiful garden: nothing taller than a cabbage usually thrives near here. It is a 'safe house', the kind that heroes of John le Carré spy thrillers make a point of establishing, a place where they can safely disappear until the heat dies down.

I feel more than usually like a spy on the run, and the garden has become an island within an island. On a damp summer's day, I sit on the veranda outside the hut in the garden with my laptop on my knee (and I come from Alabama with my laptop on my knee…) and listen to the wind in the trees; the Bosnian pine, the Himalayan cedar and the Chinese willow sounding different and very distinctive notes; and behind them, in the background, is the roar of the sea. (The branches sway on the trees but for me time no longer passes.) The garden is over-run by rabbits, pheasants, ladybirds and dragonflies all going about their business ignoring me. To them, I am not a threat, not important. It is their garden more than mine.

The sound of wind in trees is seldom as comforting as people imagine; behind its safe upper-middle-class veneer, Kenneth Grahame's Wind in the Willows is a book about outsiders and misfits, which was how Grahame saw himself despite an ostensibly distinguished career at the Bank of England. Michelangelo Antonioni used the sound of wind in trees with good effect in the film Blow-Up to create a sense of menace.

In years past, I often thought of making an expedition to the pass at the end of the Darcot valley in the Hindu Kush and pitching camp on the spot where the Victorian explorer George Hayward spent his last night. Hayward was a misfit hero of the British Empire, very much an outsider. It is hard to imagine why he should have chosen to go to that remote valley knowing that the Sultan of Kashmir, who controlled the area in so far as anyone did, wanted him dead. He probably couldn't stand the company of the British any more (he didn't even suffer sensible people gladly).

On the night in question, he sat outside his tent writing in his notebook, with a loaded revolver on the folding table in front of him, knowing all the while there were men hiding in the trees waiting for him to fall asleep, whereupon they would come out and kill him. All his bearers had left, stealing away into the night without notice (or references).

I imagine the trees at the end of his valley as willows or poplars, growing tall out of the shelter of ravine, the wind in their branches creating a strange cold rustle in the unnatural half-light of a far northern midsummer night, politely but insistently reminding him that he didn't belong there.

He fell asleep just before dawn.

Sir Henry Newbolt wrote a famous poem about the murder, which missed most of the point and deliberately turned a blind eye to much of the rest but still managed to be heroic in some of the ways that matter as well as most of the ways that don't. I was always very fond of bad Victorian verse, and I too would once have flung my empty revolver down the slope with the best of them, but I will never now go to the Darcot pass; the area is even more lawless than it was in Hayward's day, not that that would deter me, but it is physically far too tough a journey.

Beyond the garden, the cliffs are crumbling; the sea is slowly encroaching. On sunny days, I climb down the chine, ignoring the danger warnings, and walk for a mile or two along the deserted shingle beach.

I stayed in a hotel near here as a very young child, three at most, an age when memories have no continuity: disconnected fragments like the dinosaur bones occasionally revealed by the falls in the clay and mud cliffs. I remember the smell of dogs and furniture polish, and, more strongly, a view of the lighthouse framed by the bathroom window at night; perhaps also the chimes of the clock in the hallway in the early hours when I would go downstairs, stepping over the sleeping dogs and up the other staircase to my parents room to climb into their bed. I can also just about remember being puzzled by the look of suspicion – perhaps more than suspicion, more like disapproval or even fear – on the faces of the other guests. There was a polio scare at the time and my father was ill in bed, although only, as it later turned out, with shingles; it is difficult to imagine now but few other diseases have created the same climate of fear as polio in the early 1950s – leprosy in biblical times, the black death in the middle ages, the pox in the Renaissance, not many others, not even Aids. I was aware of being an outsider even then. (It was also a disease that, for some reason, particularly targeted the middle classes, already under attack by socialist taxation.)

The hotel belonged to a friend of my mother's called Graham Full-James, part of the local pre-war fast set, charming but irresponsible, or so it was said (smiling men with bad reputations). The hotel was, perhaps appropriately, not built on sound foundations and long ago fell into the sea. Perhaps I walk over its bones.

I need a safe house as I am persona non grata on this island for stupid reasons. A year ago I sat on one of the beaches a short drive along the coast and wished I was on my Greek island; the way that everyone felt constrained to wear clothes when swimming was particularly depressing.

Later my thoughts turned into a magazine article about some of the things I felt uncomfortable with at the English seaside, about England in general, and, perhaps to a lesser extent, about the life I was leading. It soon lost touch with the actual place I had been writing about (tired, I was content for the article to be on the move, on automatic pilot while I slept on the back seat for an hour or two on the road; but while I had been sleeping it had left the tarmac and transgressed into a mythological landscape – proper travel writing should concern itself with the myth behind the truth, the essence rather than the substance, but this one had broken free, crossing the barrier into the opposite lane). The imaginary inner landscape bears so little relationship to objective reality that it is best treated as fiction, a geography distinguished by mental rather than topographical landmarks.

The article was nearly right but mostly wrong, ultimately just a series of promising ideas that taken together failed to deliver; in days past, I would have worked at it, eventually arriving at an acceptable compromise: it should have been funny and light but with a few dark shadows suggesting doorways to other interpretations for anyone who cared to look for them; but it wasn't. I kept coming back to it but never made any progress, one of far too many half-written articles going nowhere on my laptop. (This laptop, the one I am typing on right now.) Nowhere, now here.

I owed some articles to a magazine and in a rash moment sent off three including that one; a fortnight later I looked at it again and emailed them to say, 'Hold off on the Isle of Wight piece; I'll send you a better version', to which they replied, 'Too late, it's in the next issue,' which was a shame because with a bit more work it might have amounted to something, but I consoled myself by thinking that not many people would read it and it would soon be forgotten, a missed opportunity rather than a disaster.

Regrettably it was a quiet week for news on the island's local newspaper (probably all weeks are quiet) and then the head of the local council took it up as a cause. There was even talk of a poster campaign to be displayed in all the pubs and restaurants with my photograph under the slogan 'Not wanted here!'

Fortunately, it does not appear to have come to anything, a three-week wonder, but when we eat out we book a table in Jenny's name.

Perhaps it is an occupational hazard. In the 1950s when covering an England football match in Rio, my godfather, the sports journalist John Macadam, wrote an article containing the assertion that, while the city had all the trappings of a sophisticated modern metropolis, 'less than a mile from Copacabana beach you can find yourself in crocodile-infested jungle', which even then was far from accurate in a purely factual sense, but he was trying to give the flavour of the place to people who would never go there, and he had allowed the words a little too much freedom to run wild; it did not go down well, questions were asked in the Brazilian parliament and an international incident was only averted by a very public apology by the British ambassador.

At the local supermarket, I look in vain for a jar of capers. The woman stocking shelves has never heard of them; I begin to explain what they are (mistakenly, I say they are the pickled half-opened flowers buds of the Mediterranean juniper, but that it's not important) and am alarmed to see an expression of horror, possibly disgust, slowly take possession of her face: 'Oh no, we don't sell *anything* like that here!' she says. I briefly consider suggesting they might profitably set up a special counter marked 'Foreign muck', but that might be too radical for them.

The following day, caught in a cloudburst in Cowes, I make the mistake of entering a yacht chandlers in search of a cheap waterproof coat. They have nothing under £150. 'I think you should try Newport,' says the sales assistant with barely disguised condescension. (Newport is where the poor people live, a town of charity shops and pawnbrokers – or so it appears subjectively.) He is seventeen at most but horribly self-assured, earning some extra pocket money in the summer holidays from boarding school. Perhaps my picture of the island wasn't too wide of the mark after all.

As we drive down the narrow, high-sided lanes, swifts fly a few yards ahead of us, like pilot fish, three feet or so above the ground following the twists in the road. They remind me of the dolphins between Crete and my island.

Chapter 8

2010

Last night I saw the old moon with the new moon in its arms – I had always assumed that was just a fanciful line from an old ballad, not something that actually happened in real life, but there it was, a harbinger of dangerous times ahead; all night on Crete as I waited for the ferry, the wind blew and the waves crashed, an angry not a glimmering sea.

Like St Paul, I am travelling too late in the year. During the day the weather is still lovely by north European standards, but at Karave port when I eventually arrived I was one of only four people to disembark. The bus driver with his shock of white hair and beard was on the quay as usual. Could he take me to Agios Ioannis? 'No. Bus problemo.'

Whenever I come here the bus is problemo, as are most mechanical things. The island is home to the most problemo collection of cars you are likely to see; doors either don't open or don't shut, rarely both; windscreen wipers are particularly problemo, not that this matters as often they have no windscreens to wipe, and no one has any reason to drive faster than ten or fifteen miles an hour.

I was not bothered by the absence of the bus as it is a pleasant walk even with a heavy pack, and hitching is always an option – almost every car stops if only to apologise for not going your way – although it cannot be relied on in a hurry as traffic is rarely busier than one car an hour.

The Joan Baez song 'We lay there by the juniper, while the moon was bright…' ran through my head as I hung my hammock under an old favourite with a view of the whole beach stretching out below; a pitch chosen for aesthetic rather than practical reasons, not a good idea at this time of year.

The beach was deserted apart from an occasional trickle of refugees from the summer heading towards the port, like Tolkien's elves on their way to the Grey Havens, and the day's sunshine was punctuated [punctured?] by fierce but brief showers, tremors before an earthquake.

When the hippies leave, the birds arrive. For a week or two, the island will be overrun with hundreds of thousands of them, part of a migration of many millions, chattering in the branches, their last stop before north Africa, or so it's said. Is it true? Most of the year you don't see any birds, certainly not the owls, falcons and choughs that Homer claimed were roosting in the trees near Calypso's cave.

On my first day, I saw two swallows, later a flock of unidentified smaller birds swooping in intricate, constantly changing formations. Perhaps, a few weeks before, they had been performing the same manoeuvres over the Norfolk Broads; soon they will do so again in the Rift Valley. Do the cranes I knew in Avila and Alcala de Henarez come this way?

Soon the plants will come back to life after their summer hibernation.

Last night, the wind was slanting in from Africa, surprisingly cold and damp, whipping up the sand and chopping the waves; perhaps the same wind that did for Menalaus's fleet.

I was woken, first by the brightness of the stars, then by a long-eared cat who had come to see what I was doing on its territory (I raised my head and the cat froze in mid tread, its front right paw three inches above the sand, eyes glinting in the moonlight), then by the lightning, then repeatedly by the cold – much colder than I had expected – then finally by the sand that drifted an inch deep over my sleeping bag. Very real at four in the morning, the end of October.

At first light, the sky is crimson. I wake again a few hours later to a perfectly sky-blue sky, bar a few torn clouds, red and painful but fast disappearing, even as I look. Then I am startled to find that while I was sleeping much of the beach has disappeared and the sea is encamped only ten yards off my hammock.

I walk along the almost deserted beach – no people, only a few goats half a mile away at the far end – and suddenly find a line of six human footprints surrounded in all directions by pristine sand: no other footprints other than mine anywhere along the shoreline. A Robinson Crusoe moment.

The sea is a constant roar, no stillness between the waves; white horses all the way from here to Crete.

The wind has changed from south-east to north to east. What does this mean? If you stand with your back to the wind and look at the clouds, it means something if they are coming towards you, something else if they are going away, but I can't remember what, and they don't appear to be moving at all despite the strong winds.

People often speculate about why Crusoe should have found only a single footprint. Professor John Sutherland says it must have been a shingle beach with just a small, almost footprint-sized patch of sand, but that is a disappointing explanation: it takes the magic out of it. And here is a genuine set of isolated footprints, not quite one but nearly, and no shingle in sight. (And how, to sidetrack slightly, did Long John Silver manage to walk along a sandy beach using a crutch? I don't think Robert Louis Stevenson seriously considered the issue.)

The sea has been making sudden raids behind my back, another game of grandmother's footsteps, encircling and swallowing large areas of beach then quickly retreating leaving only this small patch with the footprints untouched. Nearby, a substantial pool of water suddenly begins to shrink, briefly taking on the shape of a child's drawing of an elephant before disappearing before my eyes, almost with a pop, certainly without a trace. The beach does strange things at this time of year.

Last winter, a drowned dolphin washed up here, perhaps where I am standing, an unlikely troubling end: drowning is not a fitting death for a dolphin; nor is it much better for nuns, who share a certain physical resemblance with dolphins, although not the same aquatic ability. I am struggling unsuccessfully with The Wreck of the

Deutschland, drowning in a sea of alliteration. (I was shocked by the amount of alliteration on the beach.)

Crusoe spent a long time building a boat only to find it was too heavy to drag into the sea. The same thing happened to someone else in literature – I cannot remember whom and it has puzzled me all day. [I still don't know. Perhaps it was one of those 'improving' books for boys written by enthusiastic Edwardian clergymen, full of heavy handed morals, still taking up space on the library shelves when I was at school, now gone forever.]

The boat Odysseus built on Ogygia sounds suspiciously heavy from the specifications, yet somehow he had no problem in getting it afloat. (The whole business of Odysseus's journey back to 'reality' from Ogygia doesn't make sense: Homer is eager to add practical details wherever possible but none of it is believable. An excess of mundane detail often indicates a desire to disguise the dubious elements of a story, or an imaginary alibi.)

There are moments when I love the island unconditionally; I spread my arms and welcome the breeze flowing off the sea and the dappled, breeze-borne clouds. It is a place where the broken become mended, where lost limbs grow back.

Sometimes the juniper trees remind me of the wood of self-murderers in Blake's illustrations to Dante's Inferno. (I remember, I remember, where I was used to swing.) May I come here too when I die? In early years invisible except at dawn and twilight when the wind dies down to change direction. Then I will briefly share the company of strangers, never envying their ties to the material world but vicariously enjoying the stolen time when I can almost pass muster as a living person – the mysterious third who walks beside you on the road to Emmaus (or on the way to Amarillo), or with Shackleton in Antarctica, or the fourth in the burning fiery furnace – exchanging polite if slightly unsettling conversation undetected until I say something a little too strange whereupon you will turn round to find I am no longer there, leaving no footprints in the sand, or very few, perhaps one. Later I will become more sedentary, almost indistinguishable from the real trees. (Greek mythology, more that any other, is full of people turning into trees.)

Elijah sat under a juniper tree in the wilderness and prayed that he would die. 'It is enough; now, O Lord, take away my life; for I am no better than my fathers.'

And a great and strong wind rent the mountains, and brake in pieces the rocks before the Lord, but the Lord was not in the wind: and after the wind an earthquake, but the Lord was not in the earthquake: and after the earthquake a fire, but the Lord was not in the fire; and after the fire a still small voice. And the wind, earthquake, fire, still small voice said: it is the hour to be drunken, be drunken lest you would be martyred slaves of time.

The Book of Kings locates Elijah's tree a day's journey (a long day's journey into night) from the town of Beersheba in the Negev desert, not a place where you could expect to find juniper trees today but I was pleased to read that recent analysis of charcoal samples shows *juniperus phoenicia* growing in the northern Negev highlands well into the stone age, and a day walk from Beersheba is a Berber settlement called Ar'arat an-Naqab which means 'the Juniper Tree of Negev' in Arabic for reasons unexplained. The tree in TS Eliot's Ash Wednesday is usually thought to be a reference to the Elijah story although you would be exceptionally unlucky to meet three hungry snow leopards in the Negev.

The other main source of Eliot's juniper tree is the deeply odd Brothers Grimm fairy tale where it is a powerful and very sinister symbol of death and rebirth.

In the tale, an infertile wife stands under the juniper tree in her garden praying for a child 'as red as blood and as white as snow' and immediately realises she is pregnant. Near the end of her pregnancy she has a craving for juniper berries (an odd, unexplained element in the story as traditionally their most significant purpose was to induce abortions). She dies for reasons unclear shortly after giving birth to a son (the story says 'died of happiness', which is not a term much used in medical textbooks) and her last wish was to be buried under the juniper tree. A few years later, after the boy has been murdered by his stepmother and inadvertently eaten by his father, as often happens in fairy stories, his half-sister puts his bones under the tree from where he is reborn (shall these bones live?) as a beautiful bird (a 'gay and vengeful' bird spirit in Tolkien's memorable phrase) to wreak appropriate revenge on his wicked stepmother.

Elijah and his successor and mantle-inheritor Elisha were, perhaps significantly, the only Old Testament prophets capable of raising the dead.

I am not bothered about dying: in death there will be no standing orders due on the first of the month, no incomprehensible forms to fill in, definitely no deadlines. I often imagine life after death as an endless afternoon spent with old friends in the shade of a taverna, but that may just be wishful thinking.

Finding himself the wrong side in a disastrous coup, Niccolo Machiavelli was tortured by the victors or their minions and, lucky to escape with his life (if indeed he did), sent into exile in the hills above Florence in Percussina. He later described his days there in a letter to his nephew, how he rose early and worked in the fields or the woods until lunchtime, when he would eat 'such food as this poor farm and my slender patrimony provides'. Then he was off to the inn where he would pass 'a couple of hours' drinking, chatting and playing cricca (presumably a card game not a form of cricket) with the local butcher, baker and miller. Afternoons, he lay in the fields with a book. It sounds a pleasant life, and not entirely unlike mine on the island.

'When evening comes, I strip off my muddy workday clothes and put on the robes of court and palace and in this graver dress I enter the antique courts of the ancients and am welcomed by them.' (Probably sitting on his own in his room talking to the wall, holding imaginary conversations with Virgil, Dante and Petrarch.) 'I forget the world, remember no vexation, fear poverty no more, tremble no more at death. I pass indeed into their world.'

I lie awake at night, cradled by my tree and watch the stars slowly circling. The pilot star and the crooked plough hang in its branches. On damp nights it drops large salty tears on my face.

The forest breathes in sleep. In the dark, two black cats, scarcely older than kittens, glide effortlessly and silently from branch to branch like dryads. (Hamadryads are unusual in being both mortal and divine;

they die too when their tree is killed.) The Egyptians thought cats were the guardians of the dead; and they also, in some obscure way, controlled the phases of the moon.

The island's cats came from Egypt four thousand years ago, or so I read somewhere. The antiquarian Daniel George, who was a frequent visitor to my parents' house at Hampton Court, writes that no cats were mentioned in the bible. Can that be true? And is the only cat in Christian iconography the one that shared a cell with Julian of Norwich and appears in her commemorative stained-glass window in Norwich Cathedral and most other pictures of her?

Are there any cats in Shakespeare? Yes, plenty when I think about it. 'Cat shall mew and dog shall have his day,' etc. And Lady Macbeth was reluctant to let '"I dare not" wait upon "I would", like the poor cat in the adage', a favourite quote of Bertie Wooster, along with 'He asked for water and she gave him milk [the defeated general Sisera, not a cat]; she brought forth butter on a lordly dish, and while he slept she drove a tent peg through his head,' also a favourite of mine, for no obvious reason; and like Bertie Wooster I won a prize for scripture at my prep school (neither of us, I suspect, won many others). I probably still have it somewhere in storage.

Nightingales, swallows and cuckoos are mentioned almost everywhere, achieving mythic status from earliest times. But the warbler, the commonest of all the migrating songbirds in the eastern Mediterranean, is apparently entirely absent from the Bible, Shakespeare, Aristophanes and Homer, not meriting a single reference in all of Greek mythology.

Cats are ignored in Jewish dietary law even though manuals for British Army cooks serving in Palestine felt obliged to explain at length how the skinned carcass of a cat could be distinguished from anything more edible. They were regularly passed off as rabbits by unscrupulous traders who, when the cat was alive, were anxious to take their money and run before it was let out of the bag; when dead and skinned, they were less easy to distinguish from rabbits – you had to count the ribs, or something like that. ('Wery good thing is a veal pie,' said Sam Weller, 'When you knows the lady as made it, and is quite sure it ain't kittens.')

No one even knows what the ancient Hebrew word was for cat, or so it is said. Perhaps they were an unspeakable taboo because they were so sacred to the Egyptians.

Visitors to the beach are few apart from the goats (who appear often in both Bible and Shakespeare). A retired Australian professor is visiting for the day. His wife died two years ago and since then he has been travelling – Venice, Vienna, Florence, Palestine, mostly following the music. He complains that orchestras are economising by hiring cheap conductors. A very efficient German woman swims every morning at nine, no matter how cold the weather, striking extravagant poses like one of Picasso's bathers from the 1920s. 'I must swim every day,' she says. She shares a tent somewhere in the dunes with a small, balding, suntanned Greek; he doesn't swim on cold mornings, but they are clearly much in love and they walk impressive distances every day, yesterday to the far end of the island, the southernmost tip of Europe, and back.

I am going nowhere, shocked by how little stamina I have. Even the walk to the taverna and back is a struggle.

One morning, I summon up what energy I can and set off to find Pieter, following the sign to his Kalletechneion up the road towards Kastri, the island's 'capital' (a few houses among the pine trees). An hour and a half later I find another sign to the Kalletechneion pointing back the way I've come, so I retrace my steps but again fail to find it. The door to the local 'radio station' is open, the most southerly in Europe it claims (and probably the smallest); the room is pleasantly decorated with home-made furniture and a surprisingly scant amount of radio equipment, but no one is there except two men repairing the back wall which had fallen down. Yes, they know the Kalletechneion; it is nearby, but their instructions are unhelpful: 'Proceed down the road for a certain number of metres, then take a turning to the right hand.' But there are no obvious right turns. I meet the German woman and her boyfriend out on their daily walk. She gestures with her finger pointing at the sky, describing a small circle in the air: 'It is very close,' she says, but cannot be more precise. I look for its white canvas roof among the pine trees and mountain junipers but without success.

Between Kastri and the beach, the road passes a shrine dedicated to St Paul. A metal stele on the front wall (a gift from the patriarch of Constantinople in gratitude for the island's albeit unintentional role in saving the apostle's life) shows him kneeling in prayer, his hands chained, alone in an open dinghy in a wild sea beneath towering cliffs (the orthodox church was never over-literal in its iconography). A colony of very small black ants have made their home in a crack between two paving stones. I look down at them and for a moment feel like God looking down at St Paul.

A man is standing outside playing a violin very quietly, the bow hardly touching the strings, a quiet communion.

No cars pass all morning.

Unfortunately, every daily task is becoming more arduous. I cannot walk as far as I could when I was last here. Nowhere near.

When I get back, I find that the goats have peed in my space, reclaiming their territory in the best way they know. It is difficult to like these goats. I much prefer the ones I knew on more northerly islands: those on Tilos and Icaria are proper goats with an unshakably superior elegance (barely condescending to treat you as equals) and a nimbleness of foot that is almost supernatural; they cling to tiny ledges with cloven feet and dare you to follow at your peril, staring at you with 'look at me; I can do this and you can't' eyes, like a demonically possessed child turning its head round a hundred and eighty degrees. The goats on this island have none of that Mephistophilean quality; their long hair trails in the sand as they slowly plod from one place to another for no particular reason. No one would think they had the power to control the phases of the moon, or anything.

There is, nonetheless, something definitely satanic about them (possessed rather than possessors). One of them posed for Holman Hunt and others featured in the in the nightmares of Stephen Daedelus and Gustave von Aschenbach; Stephen's had human faces, muttering monotonously, and one of them was 'clasping about his ribs a torn flannel waistcoat'.

The fictional Robinson Crusoe spent his time on his island in prayer and self-improvement; the real-life Alexander Selkirk buggered the goats, which is as good an example as any of the gap between ideals and reality.

Is there a goat in a waistcoat in one of Max Ernst's pictures, like Europe After the Rains or The Temptation of St Anthony? Or am I thinking of Beatrix Potter? Ernst and Potter are probably not too far apart. Once you start looking for connections you could probably find plenty. [Or not.]

In Notes From a Small Island, the otherwise very good American travel writer Bill Bryson moaned about Potter's 'sweet little watercolours and soppy stories', but he missed the point, as do generations of parents who read the books to their children in the belief that they are straightforward, morally edifying tales; the children listening to them know better. In The Tale of Squirrel Nutkin, the squirrels gather acorns on an island in Derwentwater belonging to an owl called Old Brown, an authority figure. All the other squirrels work hard and pay appropriate respect, but Nutkin does no work, cannot resist insulting Old Brown and ends up inevitably being torn to pieces (you should ignore the cop-out last page in most of her stories; it's just there so as not to frighten the parents). For parents, this is a cautionary tale. For any self-respecting child, Nutkin is a hero and a worthy role model. The Tale of Mr Tod is a seriously violent, 'dysfunctional' story – most of them are.

'You may go into the field or down the lane, but don't go into Mr McGregor's garden,' said Peter Rabbit's mother. The world is easily divided into people who are content to spend their lives in the field or down the lane and those who get the call to go into Mr McGregor's garden, for lust of knowing what should not be known. (We lean over the basket of the balloon or stare at the view from some absurdly high place and there is always a still, small voice inside urging us to jump. What if? The terrible daring.) Life is much easier if you take the first two options: Flopsy, Mopsy and Cottontail had bread and milk and blackberries for supper, while Peter was put to bed with a dose of chamomile tea. But no one remembers Flopsy, Mopsy and Cottontail.

And Little Pig Robinson wonders why he is here, like most of us do, and why the rest of the ship's crew are so solicitous of his welfare;

then he finds out. Fictional pigs are seldom far from a realisation of existential horror. [Perhaps not the ones in Animal Farm.] Is there a connection to be drawn between Little Pig Robinson and the troubled rites of passage of Jonah and St Paul? [Probably not.]

I move my hammock to the eastern end of the beach where I can lie in the evening sun and the sand doesn't smell of goat.

A flat little bird, nondescript grey, follows the line of the shore, a foot at most above the waves, flying as fast as it can (not fast) flapping awkwardly (every bit as bad as a puffin).

A woman of the dunes called Maria is scouring pans by the water's edge. She was born in Rhodes, studied fashion at Central-St Martin's School of Art in London and now designs jewellery – she tells me the name of her website, which I promptly forget, too busy trying to remember where it was I might have met her before although I probably haven't. Later she walks off up the dune, effortlessly balancing the pans and plates on her head. Most afternoons, she practices yoga on the beach.

Perhaps we often meet people we knew in a previous life and wonder about the sudden, inexplicable rapport between us before going off on our separate ways, retreating into our separate more mundane realities. Early one morning on my way to work on a crowded London Underground I squeezed into a carriage a little too late and the closing door clipped the side of my face. The woman standing next to me instinctively reached out and stroked my forehead then immediately became embarrassed. Perhaps that was Maria, unaware that she was to know me in a future life, or a little later in this one. [More likely it was someone else, a kindly soul whom I will never meet again in this life or any other.]

Mostly, my days are spent alone, lying in my hammock and occasionally swimming in the sea. Days run one into another, morning into afternoon. You lose track of time in places like this – not that it no longer exists; rather that past, present and future exist in a more complicated order. The past has unfinished business.

On a beach like this, the Argonauts came ashore to mend their broken oars and take on water. You are woken abruptly by their voices;

sounds drift briefly from far away, and then for no good reason are inaudible from close at hand. Perhaps among the rocks the sailors found an inexplicable object and cast lots for it. A broken iPod? The left-hand arm of a pair of sunglasses? The front cover of a paperback copy of Tristram Shandy? A white plastic top of a toothpaste tube (elegant craftsmanship in some exotic ivory, a probably magical conjunction of hexagon, circle and spiral)? The youngest won it and was lost, softly and suddenly vanishing away.

I have abandoned plans to find Pieter or visit the Russians. When Sophia's taverna closes for the winter I attempt the two-mile walk to the Four Brothers in Sarakiniko but when I get there I am almost too exhausted to eat and would not have done so except that they were serving fasoulia (bean soup), the staple diet of the denizens of the Mermaid Cafe in Matala years ago.

Just outside, I find an abandoned hammock hanging between two tamarisk trees and I climb in and fall asleep until evening when I struggle back home. I don't try the journey again and for three days I lie in my hammock beside the empty glittering sea; I watch the clouds and the sunlight racing across the beach towards me but you can never catch the precise moment when shadow turns into sunlight, when sleep turns into wakefulness, when life becomes death.

This is not good.

With sickness comes a broaching of psychological defences; my mind fills with rubbish, like the lungs of a drowning man (when the dyke or the levee finally breaks); the maintenance of sanity always requires an unconscious physical effort.

I cannot look back on my past life in the world across the sea, no matter how pleasantly the memory starts, without being stopped short, brought into self-conscious self awareness, by the unwanted recollection of some gauche remark or ungenerous act, probably long ago forgotten by everyone but me; kindnesses unintentionally slighted, confidences casually betrayed, other things, all the stations of my own self-crucifixion; the past illuminated by the glow of burning boats.

Do I see a chough? At first I thought it was a seagull but it circled half a dozen times above my hammock with a hooked beak and zigzag-ending wings. I imagine a chough to be something between a hawk and a seagull, but I don't know why; for all I know they could be totally different. Swifts (or swallows or martins) dart along the beach, a few inches above the ground.

One afternoon, I watch a group of people dragging something from the far end of the beach, the first people I have seen for several days; from a distance, it looks almost as though they are dragging a lobster pot, a scene from a Frank Sutcliffe photograph or a Laura Knight painting (the light has the same liquid quality where sea, sky and beach have no clear lines of demarcation), but I never really believe that it could be a lobster pot. As they move closer, I can see they are four young men, statuesquely nude (Sutcliffe and Knight would both have approved), their bodies deep brown from the summer's sun, Maria's boyfriend's hair sun-bleached. (Does he look like I did thirty or more years ago, running along a beach beside the Caspian, with a lean, muscular body and long golden hair flowing on the wind? Possibly more than I realise.) He waves as they go past and I wave back from my hammock sick bed; two trains passing in opposite directions.

The four young men are taking turns to drag a dead goat by the horns, perhaps to dump it in one of the clefts between the rocks beyond the eastern edge of the beach. (When Geoffrey Firmin died in Under the Volcano, they threw a dead dog after him down the ravine.) The logistics of death are never good, creating, for other people, a problem of disposal. Shelley's body, famously, was burnt on Via Reggio beach, between the sea and a pine wood, which sounds romantic but the reality for the witnesses was very different.

After disposing of the goat, the young men walk into the sea to purify their bodies. Byron needed to do the same after Shelley's cremation.

My health is not improving and something has to be done; the only remedy I can think of is to go to the port where the taverna is open year round with rooms to let and where at least I will get regular meals. How much of my kit should I abandon? Both poles of my emergency tent have broken; so has the zip of my sleeping bag, and the cover has come off my copy of Tristram Shandy. In the end, I take the lot, even the disembodied cover, and I don't know why, for some reason reluctant to leave anything behind in the sand.

I walk a hundred paces, counting them out on my fingers, then look for a place to rest – not easy: I am reluctant to put my pack on the ground because I will only have to lift it up to my shoulders again: I need to find a rock to sit on with enough space behind for my pack to rest. Lines from old songs run through my head, rarely good ones but over and over, the metre always chained to the pace of my steps, accelerating as I stumble downhill, slowing almost to a halt on the climbs: 'In my yel-low jer-sey I went out on the nick/High Street Romford shop-ping ar-cade…', 'And in nine-teen for-ty-one a hap-py father has a son…'

As evening falls, barely a quarter of the way around Sarakiniko bay, just where the smell of pine trees and the electric rasp of cicadas begins to swallow you up, a bird flies leisurely, curiously, overhead and perches on a branch by the roadside; hooked beak, feathers as golden as an eagle's. (Surely they don't have miniature golden eagles in Greece? Even on this island. Or even a miniature minotaur.) The bird has a short stocky body, its head seguing without an obvious neck into powerful shoulders – I used to be taught by people who looked like that [not the feathers]. It watches me intently, curiously (more curiosity than intent) until I am only a few feet away then lazily flies off across the valley. I don't know what it is; for all I know it could be an owl; I am rubbish with birds. But it is probably not a good sign when wild animals no longer treat you as a danger.

A notice at a make-shift bus stop reads: 'Bus timetable to Karave port every [ ] minutes if there are passengers,' but there are no passengers and no bus, and when I eventually arrive the only people staying in Karave are me and the ninety-nine saints. Four miles in four hours. Not a car passed. Not a good journey.

Chapter 9

2010, 1992

I rarely walk round Sarakiniko bay by the road, preferring to scramble down the rocks to the beach to break my journey, if not my neck, at one of the tavernas; I have forgotten how special it must have been before it was wrecked. Given their architectural heritage, the Greeks' willingness to put up (and put up with) truly ugly buildings is seriously dispiriting.

The shoreline could never have been as good as Agios Ioannis or Lavrakas; the sand is much finer (not good in wind), greyer and more prone to weed, but behind it is a very deep bay of flat sand and pine trees that must once have been a perfect place to camp; when hippies first came to the island after the fall of Matala this was where they chose to live. The photographer Helen Sotiriadis spent two weeks here one summer twenty years ago, not that long ago in the history of the island, and later wrote about the 'small, hospitably bent over trees' that created 'a shady hug for our tents'; the sky was pink and lavender, the shore 'wore a lace necklace of salmon and pink crushed shells and coral', nudity was the norm and the toilet was, 'as Captain Kirk might have said, somewhere... out there'.

The stars were endless. 'My idea of nightlife was to lie on my back and watch the busy, infinitely promising sky. Sometimes I'd drifted off, and when I woke, the Milky Way had tilted. I sometimes thought I saw satellites. Sometimes I thought I'd float off the surface of the earth into space.'

Sarakiniko takes its name from the Saracen pirates who based themselves here in the bad days from the twelfth century onwards. In

1992 when Helen Sotiriadis camped here, the bay had only one building, built years before by the political prisoner Aris Velouchiotis during his exile on the island. This was where the hardest cases were sent, mostly Marxists and Jehovah's Witnesses. It is hard to imagine them socialising much, singing songs round a camp fire on the beach with a bottle of raki or two, although they probably had more in common than they cared to admit. 'The young lady of the house would serve us raki and unshelled peanuts, while we waited for her fisherman husband to come in and offer us some of the day's catch, which was... whatever, it but couldn't be fresher.'

Soon after Helen Sotiriadis' stay, a couple of rough beach tavernas appeared, then a few rooms to rent; initially they were ungainly concrete structures – those built later in the boom years were a little better, properly faced with local stone (no shortage of derelict buildings to cannibalise), but there was never any plan, certainly no streets, no pretence at infrastructure, each new building dropped almost at random among the trees; all were built illegally, anywhere their owners thought they could get away with it (usually mid way between the two most widely spaced buildings, the same formula adopted by sunbathers choosing a place to lie on the beach). Sewage drains into pits under the buildings, from there seeping away into the sand, out of mind and hopefully out of sight.

No one cares for the spaces in between: abandoned cars among the pines, piles of redundant drainage pipes and broken terracotta bricks. Sarakiniko has no roads apart from the bed of the dried-up river, tarmacked a year or two back. In the sudden fury of last winter's storms it became a river again washing half the mini-market into the sea.

Outside its brief, chaotic high-summer season, Sarakiniko resembles a ghost town from a Western film, a goldrush boom town gone bust; broken polystyrene tiles blow along the beach like tumbleweed. Vandalised signs say 'Please no nudism' (the end of Eden) but no one is swimming, clothed or otherwise.

No one has the will to stop what is happening, the constant erosion. The government in Athens does not care about beauty or anything else. In an ideal world, all the houses in Sarakiniko would be knocked down and a new village built on the rocks at the western claw of the bay. It would only need three or four streets and a square for tavernas and plane trees, the kind that might still be there half a millennium hence. But no one thinks ahead, even a few years. No one plants trees, even the ornamental cypresses, which would thrive here, as would so much else.

I sketch plans for a new village in my notebook and ponder the practicality of a waste-water irrigation system for the trees. It wouldn't be difficult, nor would it cost much, but it will never happen. Sarakiniko will just get worse and the cancer will spread. Agios Ioannis will go the same way; a metal Portakabin has already been dumped between the taverna and the sea, surrounded by blue stone chippings (not native to the island nor a thing of beauty, the stuff that builders put down when they can't think of anything better to cover the mess they've made). More will follow.

Chapter 10

2010

Another quiet day in the harbour. The sea is flat, glittering like tinsel. I am waiting for the ferry which doesn't arrive, waiting for the barbarians, who inevitably will; everybody knows the plague is coming; no one has the will to do anything about it: apathy is contagious. Nobody cares so long as they are left alone. Nobody cares until it is too late. (It is already too late. It probably always was.)

There was a brief hullabaloo earlier this year when a new policeman arrived on the island and started trying to fine people for not having number plates on their cars and silly things like that ('Who needs number plates? We know who everyone is'); after a few weeks he disappeared, and life returned to normal, for the time being. He was eventually replaced by someone who treated the job in the correct spirit – as an extended holiday.

The port is deserted, a scene from a painting by Paul Delvaux; the still sea laps against the unused harbour wall with an insistent, slightly sinister sound.

The only people staying here are me and the ninety-nine saints, whom I first encountered in the Lions taverna in Matala. The reason why they were not mentioned in the bible was because they were thirteen hundred years too late, pilgrims returning to Spain from the Holy Land. Like Paul, they were caught by the Euroclydon, but unlike him they had been able to land on the island, staying here until the storm broke twenty-four days later.

After they set sail again they realised that one of their number, St John the Hermit, had been left behind because God had made him invisible and he lived alone on the beach for reasons I couldn't follow (probably bored with the company of the other ninety-eight), later returning to Crete after throwing his mantle on the water and riding it, surfboard-like, to Paleochora – the journey took him three hours, or so it was said, much faster than the ferry would take today, were it running. (Who else threw their cloak or mantle on the water? It sounds a suitably Old Testament means of transport or method of quelling a storm, something Elijah or Elisha might have done. And what is the connection between the mantle/cloak, mantelpiece and gas mantle? Something boring like 'outer covering', I suppose.)

It is an absurdly grand harbour for such a remote, unimportant place, built regardless of expense only a few years ago when the going was good, but it is home to no more half a dozen fishing boats – little more than dinghies with outboard motors – all locals: few boats from far away have any reason to come here.

Last summer, the government in Athens suddenly and arbitrarily declared the island's ferry to be unsafe (from now on, it will only be allowed to travel twenty-two nautical miles from land and the island is unfortunately twenty-three from Crete); currently the only way to get here is by the increasingly erratic, 'twice weekly' mail boat from Paleochora. Monday's boat will definitely come on Friday, they say, but yesterday they said it would come today. No one really believes it. The sea is flat but there are rumours of storms. Or perhaps that's just another excuse; out in the bay, clear lines on the water mark where a boat passed as much as an hour or more ago, like vapour trails in the sky, the memory of water.

The expensive new crane, a modern colossus, stands idle in the sun. It can lift eighty tonnes, but nothing of eighty tonnes has ever been delivered to the island or ever taken away, or ever will be; the crane has never been used; no one knows how to use it; nobody cares.

The only thing moving in the harbour is what's left – head, tail and backbone – of the fish I ate for lunch; it stands vertically in the water, its mouth touching the surface as though gulping for air. A posse of much smaller fish are pushing it around the harbour, foraging for what I left, giving it a slightly shocking animation.

I hadn't particularly wanted to eat the fish. I would have preferred a bowl of fasoulia, but Anastasia, who runs the taverna, would have been disappointed; her son caught it this morning, and fish is not expensive on the island (it's not going anywhere), not like in the rest of Greece. But it couldn't have been fresher and it tasted like fish ought to taste but usually doesn't, particularly in Greece.

I say hello to O'Connor, a regular visitor to the island; he lives in Holland and works for a few months each year in the bulb fields spending the rest of his time walking. I was originally told he was Dutch and wondered how he had acquired an Irish accent, but he is Irish (the name is a bit of a give away). He has come here every year for the past twenty and knows every shrine and ancient pathway. For a walker he is surprisingly portly – perhaps not surprisingly: whenever I go into a taverna I find him sitting eating in a corner; he eats in much the same manner as he walks, slowly and steadily covering great distances. He liked the fish, and the fasoulia.

The distant hum of a generator is so far away that it could have its origin inside my head, tinnitis or water in the ears.

I am sitting outside the taverna under the bougainvillea. Across the bay is the little white shrine of the ninety-nine saints, Agiois Patares, its icons a profusion of tiny saints. Above it, the hills are mottled with low shrubs like elephant hide, oddly reminiscent of David Jones's landscapes of Capel-y-ffin (even more so than the real Capel-y-ffin).

Next door to the taverna, the skeleton of the 'new' hotel was abandoned long ago, its naked pillars slowly acquiring the patina of age, already resembling something from Sir Arthur Evans's Knossos with only slightly more concrete. The reinforcing rods sticking out where the second storey might once have begun are now crowned with upturned plastic bottles resembling a row of pigeons or primitive caryatids. The building belongs to a family whose members have quarrelled about how best to complete it; they would all rather watch it fall apart than give way.

A large hornet comes to investigate but I wave it away and it soon loses interest. No one pesters you on the island. No one tries to sell you anything (mainly because there is nothing to sell). Across the water in

Sfakia and Paleochora, people stand in the street and beckon you into their shops and tavernas with false professions of friendship. It is a different world.

Who has gained from the grand new harbour, the tarmacked roads, the ridiculous new amphitheatre in Sarakiniko, almost never used? They have all been paid for with borrowed EU money, all of it wasted. In the days of plenty, no one benefited; in the hard times to come everyone will lose. In one of its predictable and much publicised grand gestures the Greek government announced it would give a free computer to each of the island's schoolchildren (all three of them); unfortunately two of them don't have a reliable source of electricity in their homes, and probably never will, certainly not before they are grown up and have had to leave the island in search of work.

Anastasia's son has spent the morning repairing his moped. Unexpectedly, it bursts into life and he turns to me with a look of surprised triumph. He tests the brakes by accelerating towards the harbour's edge, fortunately without mishap, then speeds off towards the end of the jetty like Achilles in his chariot round the walls of Troy. Before long, the engine stutters to a halt, and the harbour returns to silence, unbroken and complete. Life on the island must be very dull for him.

I write all this down in my notebook. A German couple are eating in the far corner of the taverna, the only other customers. As they leave, the husband or boyfriend says: 'I thought I was the only writer on the island.' He has that elegantly haggard, large-eared look you often find in distinguished German writers. Who do I mean? As my father would famously say in such circumstances: 'Name three!' – Gunther Grass certainly, Heinrich Boll (that's just a guess), Kurt Vonnegut (German by ancestry). That will do for now.

Chapter 11

2010

Eventually feeling stronger, I track down Pieter. Like Beatrix Potter's Tommy Brock he has many homes, not all his own. Apart from the Kalletechneion where he works and sometimes sleeps, he usually spends his summers in a camp behind Lavrakas beach and his winters mostly in the taverna between Karave and Korfos whose owner, when I knock on the door, is easily recognisable from Pieter's portrait, even in the sudden darkness of the kitchen. 'Hello, I am looking for Pieter the Painter,' I say but before I have finished the sentence my eyes have become accustomed to the dark and I can see him sitting at the table.

Pieter is about to go to Lavrakas to clear the remains of his summer camp and collect a pair of small canvases from someone called Solon, so I climb on the back of his motorbike and we ride off together over the unmade roads. It feels odd riding without a helmet; I haven't done so for many years – late at night through the back streets of Tehran, three on a bike, my friend Margot in the middle; that was probably the last time.

We park where the road peters out below Kastri, near the shrine of Agios Panteleimon, and set off on foot along a four-thousand-year-old path. This is Pieter's favourite part of the island, a walk through ancient trees, passing the shrines of Agios Nikolaos and Agios Georgios, both built on far more ancient sacred sites. The path follows a stream, not yet quite flowing, more a series of still, white pools among the rocks. After the spring rains it might resemble the stream where Hylas met his naiads or Actaeon surprised Artemis and her nymphs, but not now.

The white mud in the bed of the stream is said to have health-giving properties and in summer people cover themselves with it from head to toe like New Guinea tribesmen; when it dries, they become almost invisible against the rock.

Greek islands often boast unique health-giving qualities. Odysseus Benellis, an Anglo-Greek-Egyptian textile merchant I knew in Tehran, was adamant that his home island of Leros was the only place in the world where diabetics could eat anything they wanted without getting sick. And for many years the harbour on Ikaria displayed a large sign saying: 'Welcome to the island of radiation!', alerting visitors to the attractions of the thermal spa (now defunct).

Where Pieter and I are walking was in Minoan times a town with a population of six thousand, an extraordinary number of people for such a small island, far more than it could have supported by ordinary agriculture. According to Oliver Rackham and Jennifer Moody in The Making of the Cretan Landscape, the island's main export in the Minoan era was 'hebenus', but they failed to find any convincing explanation of what hebenus might have been. (The yellow-flowered shrub *Ebenus cretica* is of purely ornamental interest and presumably not relevant.) It is a word that nearly means a lot of things, similar to the Greek word for ebony, but ebony comes from much further south. Marlowe's Jew of Malta used juice of hebene for nefarious magical purposes, John Gower called it a 'sleepi tree', and Spencer refers to 'the deadly heben tree'; the word also occurs in Harry Potter spells.

The area is still waiting to be excavated. It is one of those places where the past is very close at hand; you are conscious that just below your feet are the relics of the first and most mysterious of all the European civilisations; you tread softly because you are walking over their bones, treading on their dreams.

For a time, the path is paved with fossils – in some places almost every stone; on the Isle of Wight or near Lyme Regis you would think it a good day if you found one like that; here, there are so many it's almost impossible not to tread on them.

Lavrakas beach has that strange, hushed, slightly claustrophobic atmosphere found in many sacred places. It is not for everyone, perhaps not for me; like in an exclusive London club, I am conscious of not belonging: members only.

The name Lavrakas probably derives from 'labrys', the Lydian word for a double-headed axe, from which the word 'labyrinth' evolved via some tortuous route – perhaps because the axe could be used in two different ways, like a garden of forking paths. Its outline also resembles the horns of a bull. For Robert Graves, it is the moon of the white goddess, the two curving edges representing its waxing and waning phases.

Calypso's cave is said to be somewhere behind the beach but is now mostly buried in the sand. It was used as a burial chamber in Classical times but its treasures, if ever there were any, were looted long ago.

It is easily overlooked that Calypso was a prisoner here too, a religious rather than a political exile, one of the Titans, the family of gods defeated by Zeus in an Olympian power struggle, an overthrown Ancien Regime like the Qajars in Iran; she was still powerful in her dealings with mortals but no longer had any influence in high places. Islands were usually places of exile. St John did not go to Patmos for the sake of his health, nor because he thought it would be a good place for silent contemplation: he was sent there to get him out of the way, where he couldn't do any harm.

The name Ogygia also has Titanic associations, but while it is tempting to assume that the gods supplanted by their classical successors were those of the supplanted Minoan civilisation, this is not necessarily so.

According to Jane Ellen Harrison, classical scholar and friend of Virginia Woolf, the name Titan comes from the Greek word for white clay, and covering the body with mud was an essential element of Titanic shamanism. Much later, initiates into the Orphic mysteries at Eleusis were in some way purified with mud. Did the mysteries contain survivals from Minoan or Titanic rituals? The father (or grandfather) of Eleusis, who gave his name to the place, was called Ogygis, but I know nowhere near enough about Greek etymology to tell if that is significant.

Calypso gave Odysseus a double-headed copper axe to cut the trees for his raft – which would suggest she was an early Minoan deity, eastern rather than western Mediterranean.

Pieter says that the violinist I saw was called Darius; half English, half Persian, he trained at the Royal College of Music later joining an orchestra in Zurich before suddenly giving it all up to study Buddhism in Tibet. This year in Llasa, he assembled a bicycle from discarded bits and pieces and rode it to Delhi with his violin on his back, then worked his way busking as a street musician across India, Pakistan, Iran and Turkey before arriving on the island for the summer.

He left on the last mail boat, but, as Pieter and I are talking, he rings Pieter to say that he left a T-shirt on the wall by the harbour a week ago; could Pieter retrieve it and bring it with him when he comes to India in January? The island is still a place where things remain where you left them.

On the beach we meet a Czech woman called Euphemia or possibly Ephtemia (euphemism, ephemera, Effie Ruskin even?). This morning, for the last time this year, she covered her body with white mud; later, after it had dried slowly in the shade, she rinsed herself off in the sea; now she is rubbing her body with olive oil scented with thyme and lemon peel (Odysseus often did much the same). 'Feel how soft my skin is,' she says. Her body is deep mahogany, the kind of colour that in a painting you could only build up slowly with many layers of semi-transparent pigment. These Titanic days. The island is still a place of easy friendships.

On the promontory beyond the beach, a man called Solon has lived for twenty years in a house made of driftwood, fishermen's floats and weights, pebbles, wooden pallets, flotsam, jetsam and general rubbish purified by the sea; it started as a shack but later evolved into a proper house with several rooms but no clear demarcation between inside and out. Nothing washed up by the sea is wasted and, if no purpose for it is immediately apparent, it is put by, often for years, until a use is found or it is washed away in the winter storms, taken back to be offered to someone else. Branches are festooned with circles of twine, a lattice pergola tied with bows of old cloth; a 'dead' tree covered with fishing net becomes a giant dreamcatcher. He is, as you might expect, adept at balancing piles of stones into implausibly long-lasting sculptures.

Solon is thin, balding, austere and gentle as a monk, with something of the old Buster Keaton about him. He looks like someone who has lived a long time in silent contemplation, which indeed he has. He offers me a glass of warm white wine and continues reading a book on astronomy. Conversation is not required. Does he speak English? It is hard to tell.

His girlfriend, the lady of the promontory, has red hair almost to her waist, very like a mermaid. I do not learn her name or nationality; we communicate in smiles.

It is a very beautiful, almost absurdly beautiful, evening: a few streaks of red cloud, no wind but a luminous blue sea crashing extravagantly against the rocks.

Later, as we get up to leave, Solon shakes my hand and smiles like sudden sunlight.

Chapter 12

2010

The maze in Laurence Durrell's novel, The Dark Labyrinth, was a network of tunnels carved into the White Mountains, ultimately emerging, for those lucky enough to find the way, into a hidden valley otherwise entirely cut off from the outside world. It is not an absurd idea: there are valleys like that in the Himalayas, and I nearly went to one near Nanga Parbat, known as the Sanctuary. Another time, crossing Scotland in a light plane, we flew low over a plateau with a tarn in the middle inaccessible except by helicopter and I have often wondered what it would be like to spend a year there.

In Durrell's book, the two most ordinary but probably most believable characters – although that's not saying much – make it through to the other side where they meet an old woman who had lived there for twenty-one years, at first with three other people but two of them had tried to go back through the labyrinth and were lost and the third had attempted the climb out over the mountains and fallen to his death. The war had followed its course only a few miles away but her only contact with it was when a German plane inadvertently (but very conveniently) dropped a load of useful supplies in the valley. She never slept ('Sleep was invented for the tired; people are tired because their style of body or mind is wrong… There is no more need for sleep as there is for death'). She sat up ever night thinking suitably quiet thoughts and felt perfectly refreshed in the morning; she lived a life of idyllic self-sufficiency 'allied to the forces of nature instead of against them'; but it is all a little to easy, the necessities of life too readily available: perhaps they are all dead and are just deluding themselves that they have made it through to the other side.

Durrell would not have welcomed suggestions that he was influenced by James Hilton's Lost Horizon but the books share a similar proto-new-age philosophy. "'I remember how life was before,' pursued the old lady quietly. "I was outside everything in a certain way. Now I participate with everything.'"

In an author's note at the end of the book, Durrell claims that the story was suggested by the description of a limestone cave system near Gortyna in The Islands of the Aegean written in 1875 by the Rev Henry Fanshawe Tozer. It sounds like a spoof, and the Rev Henry Fanshawe Tozer is the sort of improbable name Durrell might have enjoyed inventing, but Tozer and the cave system both turn out to be real, although not the hidden valley at the far side.

I imagine the minotaur's labyrinth as a maze, a rat run with stone walls slightly too high to climb. A few towers rise above the walls, inaccessible from inside the maze itself but from where outsiders, people from a different dimension perhaps, can see large stretches of it, but not all. It exists in a permanent night lit by a full moon and an intense Aegean starry sky, silent apart from the distant howling of the beast who waits impatiently for your arrival. (Sometimes you can see the outsiders watching you from their towers but they never reply when you call them.) The labyrinth is not built on a formal grid with a pattern of circles or right angles like the maze at Hampton Court Palace; lines are haphazard, with no logical way out; many options are hardly options at all, obvious cul-de-sacs, a bit like life perhaps.

The maze at Hampton Court is more formal: you need to take two lefts then a right (or possibly the other way round) and then repeat the pattern until you reach the centre – this may not be true, just one of those useless or incorrect pieces of information that people store in their minds and somehow never forget while never feeling the need to verify; but it is certainly true that if you keep touching the hedge to your right or left you will eventually arrive at your destination (if you keep changing your mind you get lost), like a fool persisting in his folly, although that is a dull way of doing things.

My imaginary labyrinth exists outside time; time has stopped or has never really started; everything that might ever once have happened or might happen in the future exists side by side with equal validity, a series of parallel stationary universes where every fork in the road requires a Schrodinger-like decision.

Sometimes the minotaur is alive; sometimes the minotaur is dead.

Chapter 13

2010

The Victorian Prime minister WE Gladstone was also a classical scholar; he was most reluctant, probably correctly, to sent an army to rescue General Gordon in Khartoum but keen to support an expedition to find Atlantis. He was the first person to suggest that Homer might have been colour blind; perhaps it was the wine-dark sea that puzzled him: the sea is never the colour of wine although like wine it does become increasingly opaque the more there is of it (and perhaps drinking too much of it confuses the senses). It is safe to say that the ancients did not use words for colours the way people do today.

Blue is said to be the last colour name adopted in languages, but probably not because earlier people were unable to see it; more likely they had no need to describe anything blue – there aren't many edible things that are blue, nor many dangerous things, at least not in the Mediterranean. [Or is all of this wrong?] Does the word 'blue' occur earlier in northern rather than southern European languages?

The first use of the adjective 'orange' in English postdates the arrival of the noun/fruit by at least a century and is an approximation of the Spanish word 'naranja'. How did people describe the colour before then? Perhaps they didn't need to. Were there many orange objects before the fourteenth century? Maybe the words 'red' and 'yellow' covered broader ranges.

Perhaps orange isn't a real colour. Green is – there is a distinct point where it cannot be described as either a bluish yellow or a yellowish blue – but you can't really say the same about orange. (The taste of an egg mayonnaise and tomato sandwich is unique and quite unlike either egg mayonnaise or tomato. This is a phenomenon that I have often noticed, but it may not be relevant – it is orange though, when suitably mashed up.)

Isaac Newton effectively invented the colour indigo because he thought that the rainbow ought to be symmetrical with a distinct but minor colour between blue and purple to balance orange between red and yellow. And the words 'cyan' and 'magenta' were never needed before the advent of colour printing; magenta is named after the 1859 battle of Magenta (particularly bloody) and cyan, despite its Greek etymology, dates only from the 1890s. There are plenty of cyan and magenta flowers but they are mostly artificial hybrids of recent invention such as the large-flowered clematis, and even then plant catalogues prefer to stretch the point and call them 'blue' or 'purple'. (They never look right, resembling cheaply printed picture postcards, every bit as bad in real life as in the catalogue.) The only true species of plant with magenta flowers [or the only one that comes to mind] is fuchsia, introduced into Britain in the 1820s, but people always refer to the colour as 'fuchsia' as though 'magenta' and 'cyan' are in some way taboo. Presumably that will change eventually, but it may be a while before they become popular as Christian names [possibly sooner than we think].

Are there other colours with names still waiting to be invented whose use will eventually become indispensable, so much so that it will be hard to imagine how people lived without them? Fashion is constantly inventing names like 'taupe', but they rarely last, as is the nature of fashion.

A Voyage to Arcturus, David Lindsay's sci fi classic [or otherwise], invents two new primary colours, 'ulfire' and 'jale' – 'just as blue is delicate and mysterious, yellow clear and unsubtle and red sanguine and passionate', so ulfire is 'wild and painful,' and jale 'dreamlike, feverish and voluptuous'. [The last time I finished reading A Voyage to Arcturus I remember thinking: 'It's going to be a very long time before I want to read that again.']

All the words for colours are both adjectives and nouns, not participles or gerunds but fully paid-up nouns. Many other words are both adjectives and nouns like 'cold' ('heat' on the other hand is a noun and a verb but not an adjective). Nouns are increasingly used as verbs, an American usage possibly inherited from German, but only a few words like 'light' and (possibly) 'wrong' are equally valid as adjectives, nouns and verbs.

Is New Zealand the only country name that is also used as an adjective? You don't say New Zealish or New Zealandic lamb.

The word 'verb' is itself a noun. The French word for 'cul-de-sac' is not 'cul-de-sac' but 'impasse'. What is the French word for impasse? The word 'palindrome' is not itself a palindrome – backwards, it reads 'emordnilap', a good sounding word by any standards ('ecnalubma' is pretty good too) but not at all like 'palindrome'. When read out loud, it sounds like a word being spoken backwards, as on a tape being run in reverse, rather than one spelt backwards – are there many words that sound the same played backwards? Is there a word for them? Does that word itself sound the same backwards?

Four is the only number whose English name contains the appropriate number of letters; and vier in German, and tre in Latin, but none at all in French (quatorze-et-demi is half a character out). Perhaps the word for 'zero' should contain no letters at all, and the word for 'infinity' a infinite number, although neither would be practical. And forty is the only number whose letters occur in alphabetical order.

The word 'number' is singular, but to say: 'A number of people is waiting for you in reception' has to be wrong.

I once saw the word 'bedraggled' badly split between two lines with the hyphen after 'bed' and since then I have become incapable of reading it as anything other than 'bed-raggled'. It's a much better word, one that ought to exist, as in: 'The couple came down to breakfast next morning looking distinctly sheepish and bed-raggled.'

The Greek word for watermelon is 'karpoussi'. When Ronnie Hawkins famously said to Robbie Robertson 'You won't be rich but you'll get more pussy than Frank Sinatra' the history of rock music would have been very different if The Band had thought he was referring to watermelons. [Or possibly not. In Persia in centuries past, one of the more decadent of the Shahs had a liking for melons that only grew in a distant province in India – servants would be sent there returning on foot carrying one in each hand so as not to bruise them;

the walk took six weeks: Sinatra never lived at that style.]

The logo for Greggs bakery is the embossed braille letter G. If an 18ft-tall blind person with no sense of smell was feeling their way down the high street in search of bread they would know they had come to the right place. (Is it acceptable to use the word 'they' instead of 'he or she' when dealing with a clearly singular subject of indeterminate sex?)

Memory depends on language, without the words to define it, to fix it like a photographic image, everything is forgotten, or virtually forgotten, like events in very early childhood, like my house in Liphook. But words are not enough; they have too many gaps between them; too many things fall through.

One night under the stars in the Belouchi desert (the melon carriers would have passed this way), I could hear the tribesmen talking as I dropped off to sleep, and it sounded exactly as though they were talking English. They weren't – they were talking in Belouchi and none of it made any sense: 'What? How high is the sheep?' 'Yes so. Yes so. Come tomorrow.' English people talking nonsense would have sounded exactly the same. I thought at the time that it was just a trick, an audible hallucination caused by being half asleep, but years later I heard someone on the radio who as a child had watched the previous visit of Halley's comet while in the Belouchi desert and she said the same: that when you are falling asleep Belouchi sounds exactly like English.

Gladstone was famously reputed to chew every mouthful forty times – that was what every late-Victorian and Edwardian nanny told her charges; as a very small child Violet Asquith (who as a very distinguished old lady once sat next to my university girlfriend in the hairdressers) had lunch with him and suddenly and loudly exclaimed: 'No he doesn't!'

Is there a word for sentences that have no relation to the sentences that go before or after? And what is the word for people who think they are hypochondriacs but aren't?

When our children were small, we named a kitten Ceremony, so if anyone visited we could say: 'Come on in. Don't stand on Ceremony.' And I once knew a short-lived rock band called 'Cancelled', an appropriately punk-nihilist name, but no one turned up for their gigs.

Chapter 14

1964/1985

Late one afternoon on the school hockey field, a temporary lull in the play (or perhaps I was too far out on the wing, remote from the action), the sky overcast, the wind surprisingly warm for a winter's day, I looked down at the grass, my boots and the end of my hockey stick and asked myself why some things are remembered and others not, and, if I so decided, whether simply by an effort of will I could remember this otherwise entirely unremarkable moment for ever. And I did. Nothing else that happened that day, week or, possibly, month remains.

What else was part of that moment? Distant sounds perhaps, the noise of the captains and the shouting. The warm blustery wind is significant, the kind of wind that leans against you, politely, but insistently, nudging. Before the missionaries taught them less interesting myths, the Polynesians believed the wind was the spirit of the dead; the wind that blows on you is a different ghost from the one that blows on someone five yards away – they are just two dead people who are part of a crowd that happens to be going in the same direction.

I have twice dreamed of winds like that; both dreams were similar, unremarkable except in their lucidity which made them indistinguishable from what is usually called real life. In the first, I was in my dormitory at school and had planned to get up early in a badly belated effort to revise for an exam. Somehow I had managed to persuade myself that I could go and do some work in my study while leaving my body behind to continue sleeping. Just as it was getting light, I dragged myself out of bed, dressed, went downstairs, through the swing door and across the rose garden where I felt the warm wind leaning against me; I was half way up the steps to the cloisters where my study was the first on the left when the realisation came to me that I couldn't do this, that it wasn't physically possible, and immediately I found myself back in my dormitory sitting up in bed.

Twenty-five years later living in my terraced house in London and needing to get up early to go to work, I had an almost identical experience and was half way to the tube station, just past the Angell pub with the same wind leaning against me, before I realised what was really happening. On both occasions there was nothing to suggest that it was merely a dream. I really could have been there.

Chapter 15

2010

One evening, Pieter and I call round uninvited at the Russians, just an ordinary evening in midweek but there are eighteen for dinner, eight nationalities including the Polish photographer Andreas Kremenski – with whom I briefly corresponded a few years back but never met (he reminds me, which I had forgotten, that I had once sent a letter addressed to 'Andreas + Alexandra, Gavdos, Greece' and it had arrived safely) – the island's bus driver and the German writer from the port. He is called Hartmut Geerken, a resounding name like Antoine Doinel, Adele Domecq, Hercule Poirot or Romano Castavet, not easily forgotten, one that once started soon establishes an unstoppable momentum, like an avalanche. Ben Mallalieu? Not quite the same, but nearly.

No one is surprised to see me; it is as though I was expected, which is slightly unsettling. I am the guest of honour, much to my regret, and am therefore obliged to talk more and listen less than I would have liked, but as a result the main conversation is in English (with several simultaneous translations for anyone who needs it), the laughter only slightly delayed like in a phone conversation with a cosmonaut in space.

Hartmut's masters are James Joyce and the German Dadaist philosopher Salomo Friedlander (another fine name, although losing it slightly at the end), whom I suspect are not influences conducive to commercial success. The five-hundred-page book without punctuation or capital letters was one of Hartmut's.

Unfortunately our conversation is the kind that writers often have when they first meet, mentioning a lot of names as a means of establishing each other's working credentials without saying much of interest. (The other, even more tedious writers' discussion starts along the lines of: 'I really liked your last book; what did you think of mine?' Fortunately neither of us has read anything the other has written.)

Hartmut asks about Ted Hughes ['Who-gees'], whom, by coincidence, I had been reading that morning, the sleeping tramp in the November rain striking a chord – 'the drops on his coat flash and darken': I had noticed the same phenomenon a week ago, half asleep, watching the early morning rain on my sleeping bag, undecided whether to ignore it or crawl into my tent – but I forget to ask him about Max Sebald, whom he probably knew. (Hartmut is also an artist, film maker, actor and musician and once gave a concert in Tehran when I was living there years ago. I might easily have gone, but didn't; I often went to things like that in those days.)

The wind cradles the building, gently sculpting its contours like a potter's hands, and, not for the first time, I think I am back in the Himalayas.

The food is better than in most expensive restaurants, with a large number of mostly vegetarian dishes in no particular order, an odd but eventful fusion of East European, Far Eastern and Moroccan; prevailing flavours are ginger, sesame oil, dill and cumin. I deliberately avoid the raki, for the most part, but when I later go outside to pee in the sea, a thousand feet below, a thousand pisses deep, I realise I am drunk. How can they drink at this rate every night? If they do.

Gurdjieff's life was punctuated by an improbable and entirely unexplained series of assassination attempts, or so Gurdjieff claimed – you can never be certain if any of it was true. Researching his life, I was interested to find that one of these mysterious incidents (a bomb thrown into the cafe where he was eating) took place in Sfakia, the nearest Cretan port to the island, the port from where Guy Crouchback began his escape; Gurdjieff gave no explanation of what he was doing there. Did he have some secret connection with my island? Is that why the Russians are here? When I ask them, they claim to be unaware of the story.

I remember at some point listing my favourite Russians: Misha Tal (not Russian at all but Latvian), Andrei Rublev, Mikhail Bulgakov and many others most of whom I later forget. They drink to all my toasts except Nikolai Bukharin (perhaps they thought I said Bulgarin; but perhaps no party members are acceptable any more).

You cannot drink raki like vodka. It tastes almost the same but isn't; it catches up on you, demanding repayment at a higher rate of interest: Greek alcohol, like the Greek economy, does not inspire confidence, the road to ruin edged by vertiginous hangovers.

'You are, I think, a famous writer in England.'

'No, I am not,' I insist, but they don't believe me, unfortunately mistaking a fair assessment of my achievements for modesty.

One winter evening many years ago in a west London pub often in those days frequented by down-at-heel catholic intellectuals I fell into conversation with a shabby but kindly old man (probably not much older than I am now); he was impressed by my girlfriend who reminded him of someone he used to know, or so he said. [She had eyes the colour of opals, a usually reliable sign of bad luck; intelligent, talented and beautiful, but in every other way a disaster.] He asked me about myself, but I never asked about him: shabby old men were not important then. He was pleased I was a writer as he had spent a lifetime trying to be a writer himself without much success; my girlfriend was a painter but he found painting difficult, more and more so as he grew older. I should have noticed the high regard he was held in by his friends but I mistook their attention for good-natured affection; the old man just seemed friendly and well-meaning but of no particular relevance to my future. I mistook his modesty for failure, and it never occurred to me that here was perhaps one of the few real geniuses I would meet in my life. I never saw him again and only many years later realised who he was; very many years later. (Of course, I could have be mistaken and he really was just an old man in a pub.)

Chapter 16

1587, 1856, 1890

The Russians are for some inexplicable reason very interested in my family history, so much so that they ask me to repeat stories for the benefit of Arkady, the nuclear physicist from Chernobyl, who missed my last visit.

A select group of people have had the good fortune, or otherwise, to read their own obituary notices, sometimes like Ernest Hemingway after being declared 'missing believed lost' (I have been missing believed lost all my life); James Cameron, the old Guardian journalist and friend of my parents, found his own obituary half written in someone else's typewriter and took the opportunity to finish it off himself while the writer was at lunch. But Arkady is one of very few people to have a copy of his own death certificate. The doctor on the ward after the power plant blew wanted to go away for the weekend – possibly longer – and didn't expect Arkady to live till Monday and signed his death certificate in anticipation. No one believed he would recover and when he did they gave him stern warnings that he could never drink alcohol or go out in the sun again, all happily ignored. Now he is researching a cure for mortality, and has possibly succeeded.

Perhaps family histories had been an important element in Russian literature, the pattern repeating, each time with subtle changes like a Bach fugue, until suddenly most families had their traditions destroyed by the soviet era. A few seconds into a story, there is sometimes a murmur of approval, like in a concert by a bad American cabaret artist when the audience recognises the song. It is all very peculiar, particularly in a place where my past should have no relevance.

They ask about my ancestor Francis and the poet.

Francis had been fighting in the Low Countries having joined the expedition led by Sir Philip Sidney, the Elizabethan author of Arcadia, but none of the Russians had read Sir Philip Sidney: he is not taught in Russian universities. (They all know John Donne and the Metaphysicals: 'Even better in translation,' says Igor.)

Sidney was excessively proud of his legs to the point of refusing to wear leg armour because it would spoil the elegance of their contours. At the battle of Zutphen he picked up what should have been a minor injury, little more than a scratch on the thigh, but it festered as small wounds often did, and presently he died of septicaemia. (The Russians agree that poets rarely make good generals.) The campaign soon petered out; Francis was unwilling to return to France – he would not have been welcome – but one of Sidney's captains called Radcliffe, the son of the earl of Surrey or Suffolk or Sussex [or somewhere or other beginning with 'S'], offered him a few acres land with a stream running through it on the side of Saddleworth moor, nearly at the top of the Pennine hills in Yorkshire; there he built a small house for his family and a mill for weaving wool. (I do not tell them that my eldest daughter was conceived after a visit to Sir Philip Sidney's house at Penshurst Place in Kent; fortunately I am still too sober for that.)

My great-grandfather Henry was the thirteenth of fifteen children [possibly an exaggeration?] all of whom grew to adulthood even though just up the road at much the same time the Brontës were dropping like flies. He made an enormous amount of money, a millionaire by the age of thirty-five – he even had his own private railway station (always a good indication of wealth even though it was for work not show); unfortunately, although suitably intelligent, hard-working, energetic, decisive and modest in his personal tastes (all qualities worthy of respect), he failed to realise that most of his success was simply due to having been in the right place at the right time: he assumed it was all the product of his financial genius and he spent the rest of his life buying up failing industries he knew nothing about under the mistaken impression he would be able turn them round. The end of his life was clouded by a painful strike at the mill, his one real source of wealth.

The Russians are interested in the minor details of English industrial disputes: there haven't been many in Russia in the last ninety years. (The workers were paid a standard day rate and then so much a yard for anything they produced beyond a threshold quota; my great-grandfather installed new looms that would produce cloth faster, so he thought he was within his rights to raise the threshold, but the workers disagreed: 'Eighteen yards for nowt!' said the strike leaflets – my daughter has a copy of one in her kitchen in Dundee. It was a bad business.)

Among his many failed projects was an iron foundry, which foundered along with the rest, but with a bit of luck, if things had gone better, he could have been a front runner at the start of the motoring revolution; he might even have become another Ford or Agnelli, but he wasn't and he died a disappointed man. Success at too young an age is rarely a good thing, but then neither in the long run is failure.

Almost nothing remains of his 'empire'. After limping along for many years, the mill finally closed just before the turn of the twenty-first century and the building has been empty ever since. No one knows what to do with it, a grand but useless relic, too important to be pulled down, too big to be converted into 'luxury' apartments or put to any obviously profitable use. The only visitors, apart from vandals, are photography students from the local art colleges for whom it has become an easy but very photogenic metaphor for Britain's industrial decline. All the machinery is still there, increasingly rusty, with decades of papers and samples rain-sodden in the leaking offices.

I have (in storage) a desk and wing chair of Henry's; both have seen better days. I used to have a very attractive engraved silver and gilt cigar case of his but I gave it to my cousin for his birthday as they share the same initials; shortly afterwards, his house was burgled and it was stolen, as is the way with things.

Olga, who writes clever, Borges-like short stories, asks about the car, a story she remembers from my last visit. That was about my great-great-uncle David who was less modest in his personal tastes and owned what was possibly the first car in Yorkshire. A week after he bought it he went to play at Meltham Golf Club, parking the car outside the clubhouse at the top of the hill. The caddies had never seen anything like it and climbed all over, one of them accidentally releasing the handbrake so that the car slowly gathered speed down the hill before crashing through the wall at the end into a quarry. It wasn't insured. The story always seems to me like a metaphor for my family history.

The Russians are less impressed by my favourite story about my great-great-uncle David: a friend committed suicide and the local chapel refused to bury her in consecrated ground so he took an axe, smashed down the door, conducted the service himself and had her buried in the churchyard. Perhaps that was how the rich and powerful have always behaved in Russia, before and after the revolution.

I try to explain, perhaps not well, the crisis of confidence in the English upper middle classes in the first half of the twentieth century, how my grandparents had devoted their lives to public service with the inevitable waning of the family fortunes. The Russians would have had much worse to put up with at the time. I also tell the story of my father's cousin Percy, never a good sign, always a clear indication that I have drunk too much.

After centuries of reasonably honest toil (the name Mallalieu sounds posh but isn't) – not greatly rewarded but, as was often said, no Mallalieu ever doffed his cap to bishop or squire (or to employer or landlord) – followed by sudden unexpected wealth, the family produced a single brilliant generation, as many similar families did, almost all of whom achieving or nearly achieving enormous success in many very different fields, although rarely adding much to or noticing the dwindling family fortunes. Percy was the cleverest of all of them and should have been the most successful, the one that everyone now remembers.

At school, my school, the school we all went to, the headmaster said that Percy was the best mathematician they had ever had. (His elder brother Maurice was not as clever but was later perhaps unlucky not to win a Nobel prize.) Percy was awarded the top scholarship of his year to Oxford University but the war intervened and he enlisted, stupidly like all the others. I have a photograph of him sitting outside his tent, looking younger than his eighteen years, very good looking, very like my father at that age, perhaps even more like me at that age –

sometimes I look at the photograph and I see myself looking back. Within a month of enlisting he was sent to the front and a week later was trapped for three days under fire in no man's land; on getting back to the lines he was asked what had happened to his platoon and when he said he had left them behind he was given a summary trial and shot. Coming from what was then considered a 'good' family, the matter was hushed up, the official report inventing some story about him being killed when going back to save a fellow officer even though he had been warned it was hopeless.

His commanding officer's decision to shoot him would have been a severe over-reaction even by the standards of the time, and he as much as anyone would have had an interest in hushing the matter up.

One night a year or so later, Percy's younger brother Pat was out in no-man's-land as a spotter for an artillery regiment; a German offensive was expected in the morning – everyone said so, no doubt about it – and he spent the night knowing he would be caught in the first wave and they would take no prisoners. For some unexplained reason they never came (still a mystery to military historians) and he spent the rest of his life failing to come to terns with the anticlimax.

After the war, he went back to his mother's – my great-aunt's – house in North Oxford; he and two friends borrowed her attic as an office and each wrote a book: one had his published but shortly afterwards died of tuberculosis; the second was the novelist Joyce Cary who went on to great things and still probably deserves to be read, although possibly isn't; but no one wanted Pat's book – the market was already knee deep in first-hand accounts of the trenches – so he gave up his ambitions to be a writer and became a schoolmaster. (Forty years later, after he retired, he tried again and this time his book was published and has become something of a classic.) Another cousin, Donald, joined the Royal Flying Corps and became a celebrated first world war fighter pilot and air ace, ending his career as an Air Chief Marshall in the RAF. There is no way of predicting who will be heroes and who won't. (But gentle people are just as good people as heroes, probably better.)

There are other stories, but only ones I tell when very drunk.

Chapter 17

1962, 1936

This not one of them; it is something else, a slight change of direction while not entirely changing the subject.

I once met the 'Moors Murderers', Ian Brady and Myra Hindley, or quite possibly I did nothing of the kind and the people I met were an entirely blameless couple who just happened to be wandering around Saddleworth Moor on a hot afternoon in the early 1960s – it is impossible to tell which (as I grow older it becomes increasingly difficult to be certain about much: things that once were important no longer matter; quickly forgotten incidents suddenly years later burn brighter for no obvious reason).

On that particular afternoon, I was a young teenager staying with my uncle and aunt at Larkwood, the family home, or the latest incarnation of it, the last house on the edge of the wilds. The future Leader of the Opposition, writer, historian, family friend and all-round good person Michael Foot stayed at Larkwood when he was an undergraduate at Oxford and much later wrote about 'the old Huguenot house in the hills', but his memory had misled him and the place where he stayed was then little more than thirty years old, although it would have looked older. It had been built by my grandparents only at the turn of the century, an ostentatiously grand stone house with a large conservatory and fake castellations, a beacon of late-Victorian/early Edwardian certainties anticipating an ever more prosperous future which, after the first world war, failed to materialise.

When my grandmother died in 1936, my eldest uncle, who had been planting cotton in Egypt, came home to live in the 'old' house and run one of the last of the family mills. He was a decent, old-fashioned person, a Tory patrician of the old school; when in the 1950s it was rumoured that one of my other uncles might be offered a peerage he was quietly but deeply shocked to learn that someone other than 'the head of the family' could be entitled to call himself Lord Mallalieu.

My aunt, who was half Italian or Greek or Coptic, and always one of my favourite people, found the old house cold and impractical, and most buildings look ugly thirty or forty years after they are built, out of tune with the changing spirit of the times. Very soon the old house was pulled down and replaced by something that by the time I first knew it in the 1950s was itself looking ugly. The widely accepted verdict, the one I inherited, was that the new house was characterless without a single good room apart from the hall and the staircase, my uncle having hired the local mill architect who was only good for designing factories, or so it was said.

My father, who was the third son, loved the 'old' house. Once playing hide and seek with his nephew and niece he chose a hiding place they never discovered; even in the 1960s, when they were long grown up, they would ask him where he had been hiding but he said he would never tell them, and he never did, a small secret shared only by him and the old house.

Now, looking back at what I remember of the 'new' house. I can see traces of art moderne in the use of metal window frames and possibly echoes of Mussolini's North African architecture, understandably ignored for many years but now beginning to be highly regarded.

On the hot summer afternoon in question, I had gone for a walk on my own and found a broken cattle trough; the pin holding the ballcock had sheared and the pipe was spraying water over the moor. I was busy mending it with some wire and baler twine when I gradually became aware of two people standing close by watching me – I hadn't thought that there had been anyone within half a mile, at least.

The woman had blonde hair, possibly dyed, and wore a cotton dress, white with a floral pattern, and a thick, dark leather belt; the man had neatly combed (Brylcreemed?) dark hair and a suit with all three buttons fastened. Do I really remember this, or is my mind making up facts to fill a vacuum? I do remember clearly that the woman asked what I was doing and when I explained she said: 'That's very clever of you,' and then added: 'We're going for a picnic. Would you like to join us?' The man said nothing, standing further back but he appeared to be in control, pulling the strings.

I thanked them politely for the offer but said I had to go home and off I went, and then completely forgot about the incident. The memory remained buried throughout the trial and the subsequent notoriety until one afternoon in 1986 or 7 when I was crossing Grays Inn Road in London on my way back to work and suddenly, for no particular reason, remembered it all and thought 'Oh'.

Chapter 18

2010

One morning, at first sight no different from any other, the harbour wakes up, suddenly full of people like a Thomas Hardy town on market day. Where do they all come from? There cannot have been that many people on the island. They arrive in early summer on the boat and then for months are never seen again, reappearing unexpectedly in autumn to take the ferry home, knowing somehow instinctively that today is the day.

The arrival of the mail boat is street theatre for the locals, for those who are neither coming nor going, a distraction from the boredom endemic in small islands, something unnoticed by occasional visitors. The bus driver is there even though his bus is, as usual, elsewhere. Solon and his girlfriend arrive in a surprisingly smart new dinghy to collect their monthly supplies ordered by mobile phone from the supermarket in Paleochora.

Today, many more people are leaving than arriving. Ephtemia carries a heavy pack, still barefoot but otherwise dressed in a loose (random) assortment of silk, cotton and cheesecloth in faded purples and sun-bleached greens, and broideries of intricate design; but she looks older, less immortal, already part of a different, less interesting reality, the gold fading into lead.

The Amazonian explorer Colonel Percy Fawcett described the town of Rurrenabaque, where many of his early adventures began or ended, as 'a dismal heap on the way into the jungle, a metropolis on the way out'. (And it still is, although now a centre for backpackers rather than outlaw gunmen and riverboat chancers.) Paleochora and Chora

Sfakion, or wherever you are lucky enough to get a boat to or from, have much the same dual identity. Helen Sotiriadis found her return to civilisation a shock after only two weeks. 'Why was the ground covered in asphalt? Why did people live in cement cages? Why couldn't you just go from point A to point B in a straight line? Why did you have to follow a road (you don't do that in the sea)? Why did trees have to be jailed in a boxed-in patch of ground? Why did people wear all those clothes? How did they breathe? Why was everything so ugly?'

She never went back to the island; the first wave of ugly houses in Sarakiniko were already being built and she knew it would never be the same again.

Chapter 19

1982

One autumn afternoon, waiting for the Magic Bus in an Athens back street, I was surprised to hear an Irish voice very close behind me say quietly: 'Please don't move. Just stand where you are.' So I did. Someone was hiding in the shadows of a doorway almost invisible only a few inches away. If he hadn't spoken, I might never have known he was there. When the bus arrived, we went on together and sat together at the back and talked to each other in a desultory fashion through the inevitably tedious journey, my secret sharer and I.

The Irishman had been working on Crete, labouring on a building site; he had made a local girl pregnant, her brothers had come to remonstrate and in the resulting disagreement one of them had been stabbed, perhaps fatally. The Irishman had walked all night across the island to a port where he hoped they might not expect to find him.

He needed to get out of Greece in a hurry, but when our bus stopped late at night at the Yugoslav border and the passports handed over, the wait was longer than expected; then the two of us were ordered out of the bus – just the two of us out of thirty-five passengers; I had to take the Irishman's arm to stop him from stumbling down the steps.

There had been bad moment earlier in the journey, particularly when a police car overtook us with its siren blaring (looking for someone else or going home for tea), but mostly it had been a slow build-up of dread as the day darkened and we neared the inevitable collision with the border: that was where he would be found out, if anywhere, where 'they', whoever they were, would be waiting for him. The driver collected all the passengers' passports and took them to the customs office, and much later an official came out and summoned just the two names, the pronunciation at first unrecognisable (a curious mixture of awkward embarrassment and theatrical flourish, with a small but definite undertone of contempt) – 'Mall-al-eee-ow! Mock-a-leesi-ou' – then a sudden sickening realisation, a dreadful awakening, the comical nature of the pronunciation adding exponentially to the horror (experienced only at second hand because I surely had nothing major to worry about; I could not remember having done anything particularly wrong, but things often have a habit of happening to me without my noticing, without fully understanding the consequences; and fear is always contagious. Few people who have been to an English boarding school can entirely forget the sensation of slowly becoming aware that something wrong has been done and someone is about to be punished for it, and, even though you have no idea what it is, you have the dawning certainty that that person is you.)

Amazingly, neither of us had any real cause to be concerned; it was just one of life's jokes, the kind it likes to play at bad moments: we were taken to the office, told to sign incomprehensible pieces of paper and then fined ludicrously small amounts of money (less than a pound each if my memory is correct), the Irishman for over-staying his visa, I for forgetting – or not bothering – to go through customs when I had entered in the country.

He, the Irishman, was very relieved to cross the border, a bad business best forgotten.

Chapter 20

2010

When Odysseus rounded Cape Malia driven by the storm, he passed out of the known world. Between then and when he arrived home in Ithaka nothing can be said for certain about where he went, and even the 'real', present-day Ithaka sits uncomfortably with Homer's description of it as the most westerly of its group of islands. He might have meant the most westward facing, the others having their harbours and main towns on the usually more sheltered eastern side, or he could have meant somewhere completely different, or he was talking complete bollocks.

None of the places Odysseus visited in between are remotely plausible, but ever since Schliemann supposedly struck lucky at Troy people have been unable to resist having a go at plotting his likely itinerary. This is an amusing and increasingly addictive academic game, but without any real point, even assuming it isn't an entirely fictional story, which it certainly is. You are never going to come up with a correct answer: it is a jigsaw puzzle with half the pieces missing, and hopelessly muddled with pieces from other puzzles.

You cannot trust local legends. Most Mediterranean caves are claimed by someone as the home of Polyphemus, including the one just across the water from my island at Sougia (hardly surprising, of course: in the early nineteenth century when rich explorers from the north started looking for Homeric connections the local inhabitants were unlikely to say: 'No, there's nothing of that sort here. Why don't you try twenty miles down the coast and take your money with you?').

Many places look right – just about everywhere in the right light.

One autumn years ago (1982, the year I met the Irishman), I sailed an old gaff cutter from Corsica to Athens and every new place I went to was like treading in Odysseus's watery footsteps only a pace or so behind. Once on the early watch I saw the long-dormant volcanic island of Ustica floating in the dawn light and thought it had to be the Island of the Winds, or the Siren's rock, or Circe's island or somewhere. Later, in the straits of Messina I climbed the mast to look for Charybdis (it was actually marked on our marine charts) and there it was: a patch of slowly revolving still water.

For Ernle Bradford in his optimistically named Ulysses Found (in storage along with all my other books) the Land of the Lotus Eaters is Djerba; Polyphemus's cave is in southern Sicily; the Laestrygonians in Bonifacio; Circe's island is at Cape Circeo; Scilla and Charybdis in the straits of Messina; the Island of the Sun on the east coast of Sicily; Ogygia, Malta; and the land of the Phaeceans, Corfu (Ustica was supposed to be somewhere): it is a conventional and generally plausible interpretation, all very sensible and shipshape. Bradford's views are usually worth respecting, despite his low opinion of the Matala hippies – he knew the sea and its harbours better than most writers and historians; once, in a two-year spell in the Mediterranean he spent only two nights ashore, which has to be impressive. But he admits that his itinerary has a couple of serious inconsistencies: to reach Bonifacio, Odysseus and his crew would have had to row for six days and nights across open sea in what they must have known to be entirely the wrong direction, and if Malta was Ogygia Odysseus could not have sat on the beach staring out across an empty ocean without seeing Gozo only a few miles off.

Worse, on Circe's island Odysseus climbed to a high point from where he could look out at the sea in all directions – it could not have been a promontory like Cape Circeo. Homer is probably precise in his use of the word 'island', and, in contradistinction, when he just says 'land' he probably means somewhere attached to the mainland or a small part of a much larger island: the land of the Lotus Eaters is probably not Djerba, nor is the Island of the Sun part of Sicily. I have a book by a couple of Germans (names forgotten, also in storage) who suggest that the land of the Phaeceans spanned the instep of Calabria which makes some sense although they concede that in order to get there Odysseus would have had to be taken the wrong way by the current through the Straits of Messina (or something like that). And he would never have been able to sail from there to Ithaka overnight (it took me three days). Perhaps it is significant that Odysseus was asleep; sleep may have a different or deeper meaning in the Odyssey, when time passes at a different rate; and, of course, there may have been times when he was technically dead without realising it, not least when he was washed up on Ogygia. (It happens to a lot of people, I suspect, persisting with all the tedious chores and worries of their old lives, trying to keep body and soul together, without realising that none of it is strictly necessary.)

Even the usual attribution of Scilla and Charybdis to the straits of Messina cannot entirely be trusted as a fixed point from which to plot the rest of the journey. Of course geography changes and the 'whirlpool' now called Charybdis might once have been a serious danger, but according to Homer it was difficult to steer a path between it and the coast where Scilla lurked; the straits are now the best part of a mile wide and the only real danger to sailing boats comes from the ferries that speed from one side to the other and don't get out of the way for anyone – no concept of sail before steam – not a problem in Odysseus's time.

Tim Severin in The Ulysses Voyage puts the Land of the Lotus Eaters further east on the African coast directly below Crete, Polyphemus's cave near Elefonisi and the Island of the Wind is one of the little islands to the north west of Crete where in classical times ships could be held up for weeks waiting for it to blow in the right direction. He finds a suitable bay for the Laestrygonians in the Mani; Scilla and Charybdis are put in the narrow strait that once existed between Lefkas and the Peloponnese (and he even finds a cave on the mainland called Skilla), all of which is promising except that, like attributing the land of the Phaeceans to Corfu, as most people do, it is hard to believe that someone like Odysseus who thought little of sailing from Ithaka to Troy should get hopelessly lost so close to home (the Phaeceans knew his name because of his deeds in Troy but not because he was king of the next-door island). Severin suspects that the Odyssey is a combination of two incompatible journeys and it's hard not to agree; he also accepts that it is impossible to fit Ogygia into either of them.

Ogygia is a place apart, certainly very remote. Very few islands in the Mediterranean are entirely out of sight of land or other islands, but Ogygia was. Hermes, who presumably could fly quite fast, pointedly complains about the monotony of his journey there over the unbroken waves, yet Odysseus supposedly managed to float there in seven days clinging to the wreckage of his ship.

Ogygia was also very small. When Hermes arrived at Calypso's cave the scent from burning juniper logs wafted far across the island; its only inhabitants were Calypso and her nymphs – she had no contact with either men or gods – and the text only mentions one beach, where Odysseus sat day after day with tears streaming down his face staring at an empty ocean. But despite being on such a small island, Calypso's cave had four streams running round it, supporting a flora of alders, poplars and cypress, grapes, iris and wild celery. Green islands can be found in unlikely places in the Mediterranean: Tilos, for example, has many springs, the water falling as rain far away on the mountains of Asia Minor and travelling underground in aquifers before resurfacing there, while nearby islands are barren, even those almost directly between Tilos and the mainland; water moves in mysterious ways. But no island in the Mediterranean is a mile or two at most across and forty miles at least from any land but with enough spring water to feed proper streams and sustain a deciduous green landscape; nowhere remotely like it.

Ogygia is never going to fit in anywhere in a strictly geographical sense; and if you accept that, it can be wherever you want it to be. It belongs entirely to the mental rather than the topographical landscape.

An American travel writer (name in storage) sailed past my island on a troopship during the last war and suddenly felt with unshakeable conviction that he had discovered Calypso's island, no evidence cited or desired ('Every small island sighted by the man on watch/ Is the Eldorado promised by Destiny'); it would be good to feel the same, but part of me, the part that went to school and was taught to think logically, insists there should be some proper evidence apart from the frequent references to juniper trees in the text, and the prevailing air of magic. I discussed the problem with Pieter who once painted a memorable picture of Odysseus swimming towards the island; he said that what convinced him was Homer's reference to the sharpness of the rocks when he reached the coast, but when I checked with the text I found that was a different shipwreck, the one when Odysseus washed up on the land of the Phaeceans.

The 'real' Ogygia really was Tir na n'Og, lost somewhere in the Celtic twilight. (Gog and Magog, Mrs Ogmore-Pritchard, Ogden's Nut Brown Flake, Noggin the n'Og. No obvious connections yet.)

Chapter 21

2010

My younger daughter has spent the summer on Shetland. Fragments of messages come back to me: she has seen an otter; they tried again to walk to the lighthouse but never got there because, as before, someone they met on the way invited them for a drink or a meal. Her boyfriend was born there and knows all the islanders.

Would it be a bad place to live for half the year? Mid-December to mid-March on Shetland (three months of winter would be enough to give meaning to the rest of the year, probably more than enough), mid-March to mid-June under a juniper tree in Greece before the crowds arrive, mid-June to mid-September in an endlessly light Shetland 'summer', then a long Greek Indian summer and autumn followed by a dark northern winter again under the Northern Lights. It isn't an impractical journey: a short ferry to Kirkwall, an overnight ferry to Aberdeen, an overnight bus to London, bus to Gatwick (or just a flight from Aberdeen), flight to Crete, bus to Sfakia, Sougia or Paleochora, ferry to the island, three rough nights at most. I could still manage that.

All we would need on Shetland would be a one-room shack by a beach with a corrugated iron roof (so we could hear the rain), a glass lean-to on the seaward side to live in most of the time watching the sea, the stars and the northern lights. A small wind generator should provide just enough power for a laptop and a record player (vinyl not CD) playing Dark Side of the Moon, Shine On You Crazy Diamond, Blue Note Jazz (and possibly Bach fugues and Mozart violin sonatas). The waves on the sea would have a different pitch, or perhaps a different rhythm (I know sod all about music) requiring a different kind of music from what I would listen to on my Greek island. In the sixties I knew people who experimented with strobe lights to slow down or speed up the alpha rhythms of their brains. Perhaps alternating between two different seas would have a similar effect.

No bills, no standing orders, no newspapers, television or radio. Definitely no car. No machines to go wrong. My experience of machines is that they cost an awful lot of money, give very little real satisfaction and surprisingly little practical assistance but the moment you have to rely on one it lets you down.

Living for nothing. Water from the stream, firewood from the beach or peat cut from the moor. (Probably cut by other people as a favour: how do you even start to cut peat and produce something usable as a fuel?) A walk along the shore in the hour or two of midwinter half-light, collecting the day's offerings from the sea. (Northern beaches should be much more productive than those in the Mediterranean, a small compensation for the coldness of the water.) A walk to the pub in the still moments between day and night when the wind dies down before changing direction (if it ever does). Occasional evenings listening to live music with single malts, ceilidhs in over-lit, under-decorated village halls with bad acoustics before a long stagger home to the shack in the wildly windswept dark.

But the reality of the place may, of course, be very different. Sadly nowhere in Scotland is really like The Wicker Man, much though I would like it to be.

My daughter is impressed that Hartmut used to play music with Sun Ra, who is apparently highly regarded by her musical friends at Dundee University, but Salomo Friedlander may be a step too far into obscurity. There is nothing essentially wrong with obscurity. I once heard of a sculptor who made a series of welded metal boxes that were impossible to open without destroying their contents; inside, he placed objects that only he would ever know about. There is no reason why writers should not do the same, although it is probably not a good idea for philosophers. [Heidegger might have disagreed, as certainly would Gurdjieff.]

Pieter may have found himself a new home, an old house to rent near Kastri with enough space for the Kalletechnikon and a vegetable patch. He had talked of buying some land and building a house from discarded plastic bottles, but there were too many obstacles. 'Once you buy, the government becomes interested; it wants taxes.' Greek property law is a disaster and the EU-funded years of unearned prosperity have left people with a hopelessly misguided idea of what anything is worth.

'If you own nothing, they can't take it away from you,' he writes.

I am playing with the idea of a building a wooden shack on wheels, on a caravan frame or a low trailer, with a veranda that folds down at the front, and a roof that pulls across above it. It would fail to pass any highway regulations (not that there are any on the island) but it could be moved around, towed slowly behind a car. I could park it on the beach at Korfos without anyone complaining (for a while at least), by the rocks at Agios Ioannis or under the trees where the road peters out near the shrine of Agios Nikolaos on the magical path to Lavrakas. And I could leave it somewhere safe when I wasn't there.

Unfortunately, the best places to live on the island are a long way from anything resembling a road; I would really need to build a permanent shack, just one room with a veranda, but it couldn't be left empty for long – if I did, it might not be there when I got back, or someone else might have moved in. It would be a shame to have to padlock it: every time you lock a door, part of you becomes a prisoner (people are owned by their possessions). I could leave a notice inside saying: 'I am sorry I was not here when you called. I will be back shortly but you are welcome to live here in the meantime, and feel free to leave it as untidy as you found it.'

A proper roof offering protection against winter storms is pretty much essential; a wood-burning stove for cooking and heating would be a useful luxury. As would a wooden floor – sand quickly becomes tedious. Unfortunately, the list goes on, and once you start there is no stopping it. I read about someone who lived in Matala in the old days who was lucky enough to find a room to rent with a cold-water tap on the wall outside; suddenly everyone else wanted one too (a fridge would be next on the list); what were once luxuries quickly become essentials. It is a slippery slope. The world, rex mundi, will always try to drag you back if you let it. Comfort is always the enemy of freedom. (I get more Cathar as I get older.)

The hut could be built somewhere unobtrusive, where no one would have any sensible reason to object (I fear they would though), out of the way under a tree on the road to nowhere on a slope too steep for a tent, sheltered from the worst of the weather but hopefully with a clear view of the sea. I draw designs for it in my notebook, a series of cantilevered, interlocking levels, with steps leading up to a veranda, another step up to the hut floor, with the raised sleeping area beyond that, the whole structure diagonally braced to stop the roof flying off in a high wind. It wouldn't need to be big, no more than six foot by eight with a four by eight veranda, just enough space for a bed, bookshelves, a few cupboards, somewhere to hang clothes and store food. The Russians could build it for me in an afternoon.

On the bookshelves I would keep The Way of Zen, Hunger, Zarathustra, Four Quartets, Labyrinths, Kafka short stories, Nausea, The Odyssey, Gulliver's Travels, Walden, Diary of a Nobody, Portrait of the Artist, Rings of Saturn, Alice in Wonderland, I Ching, Wind in the Willows, The English Assassin, Lanark, The Dragon Book of Verse, Paradise Lost, Tibetan Book of the Dead. That would do for a start, probably more than enough. There is no point in having a Kindle with hundreds of books – you end up reading none of them, or none of the difficult ones, and it is just another thing to go wrong, be discarded and confuse the Argonauts when they pick it up.

I have recently discovered The Land of England by Dorothy Hartley, an academic social historian but not afraid to write beautiful sentences (probably now very unfashionable). I am particularly taken with the sections on escapists and hermits, the people of the middle ages who, rejecting or rejected by the mainstream world and its ethic of kill or be killed, went to inhabit the wild places and 'no longer desired involvement in the herd'. The escapists were mostly peasants who reneged on their feudal obligations; the hermits were more often damaged refugees from war, many of them former soldiers, 'simple, tired men who built themselves serviceable huts by some spring of fresh water and lived as best they could'. To be a hermit was, at first, not a specifically religious vocation, although nothing in the middle ages was ever entirely religious or entirely secular, And disillusioned returnees from the crusades might have been familiar with new ideas about philosophy, theology and medicine, exotic to people who had never left the straight confines of home. They became wild men of the woods like Sir Lancelot (and in the middle ages there was also no clear distinction between madness and religious enlightenment).

I wish I could have been taught by someone like her when I read history at university, but the first lecture I went to was a very dry exposition on the pipe rolls in the See of Canterbury in the fourteenth century – tithe records, land deeds, that sort of thing – and my only reaction was: 'What is this shit?' and from then on there was no looking forward, although in all probability I had already closed my mind to it; for all I know, the pipe rolls could be a treasure trove of interesting information, every bit as productive as Dorothy Hartley's sources.

I begin to imagine myself as an ill-made, misfit knight shipwrecked on his way home from the crusades (or jumping ship, fed up with the company of his travelling companions) and choosing to spend the rest of his life on Agios Ioannis beach under a juniper tree, walking every morning along the sand (leaving only a few footprints behind him). Perhaps I should invent his memoirs (another apocryphal autobiography), taking the travels of my non-ancestor Sir John de Mandeville as a starting point. In spring, autumn and winter the beach would have been exactly as it is now and every bit as magical. I wouldn't have to change much.

At the end of the film of Henri Charriere's Papillon, the hero is shocked that his old friend and would-be fellow escapee, played by Dustin Hoffman, has given up on their fight for freedom; he has built a little hut overlooking the sea, planted a few vegetables, and that is enough for him. Papillon cannot understand it and tries one last, successful attempt, floating away on the tide on some inflated sacks (an Odysseus-like undertaking), a risky business at best. Perhaps he was driven by sexual desire; if Devil's Island had been invaded by hundreds of beautiful people every summer he might have found it a more congenial place.

St Jerome the hermit was also tormented by desire (as, famously, was WE Gladstone, and probably most people). Perhaps that is the symbolic meaning of the lion in St Jerome's iconography, although the one in the Dürer engravings looks a particularly benign, well-satisfied creature. (The girlfriend of Solon the hermit beyond the beach at Lavrakas has hair the colour of a lion's mane. If St Jerome had spent his time in the wilderness with someone like her rather than with an actual lion he might have been a lot more cheerful, although they probably wouldn't have made him a saint.)

Gladstone kept his passions at bay by cutting down trees, even well into old age, happily oblivious of the Freudian implications. After Freud, people became much more inhibited. Victorians at breakfast would freely discuss their dreams of the night before unaware of the likely symbolism. William Morris wrote a poem about a king on his wedding night who goes to his wife's bridal chamber to claim his prize but is dismayed to find a monstrous serpent silently arise between them (the silence of its movements is particularly shocking). He reaches for his sword, but his scabbard is empty; his bride looks at him with undisguised contempt and he slinks off and lies outside her door, howling like a dog, while she is presumably ravished repeatedly by the serpent. People don't write things like that any more. (I may be exaggerating this story; it is a long time since I read it; it could be completely different; I might have made it up entirely.)

Pieter writes again to say he had enjoyed reading Bulgakov's Master and Margarita so much he had immediately started reading it all over again, an unheard of thing for him to do. I had been about to do the same when Pieter borrowed my copy, leaving me alone with Gerard Manley Hopkins and a disintegrating copy of Tristram Shandy.

Pieter doesn't say whether he managed to rent his house or if he is still planning to get to India next year.

Chapter 22

2010

What would I miss about England if I never went back? Most of the good things are just an illusion, but they never entirely lose their power over you; they can bring you back with a twitch on the line (a hook in the lip) though you travel to the far end of the earth.

Once very sick, crashed out in a cheap Afghan hotel (a charpoi in a corridor), I re-read the Scholar-Gipsy in a tattered paperback of English verse and wished intensely I could be back in England trailing my fingers in the Thames at Bablock-Hythe – a serious attack of homesickness – but when I got well and went 'home' I never thought of going to Bablock-Hythe. I never even looked it up on the map to find out where it was. It isn't a real place, not in any real sense, not one that matters, part of the mental rather than the topographical landscape. (If you found somewhere called Avalon on a road map it would probably turn out to be no more that a motorway service station and a run-down superstore for Land of Leather.)

I always looked forward to the changing England seasons, mainly because the next one can't be any worse (but it usually is). This is, of course, written mostly from a city perspective: out of town, English seasons are much better (and in some ways worse, of course, but always more significant).

Summer is usually too cold, too wet or unpleasantly humid, the wrong kind of heat, at best three fine days then a thunderstorm. It is many years since I last played cricket, sheltering under an oak tree in a cloudburst, but never forgotten is the smell of sudden rain on dust and white flannel (more cream than white, and the grass and ball stains never entirely eradicated in the wash, a palimpsest of past matches), but I never will again. And no one wears real flannels any more: it is all synthetics now (and with a large logo down the leg).

I might miss the cloudless, sharply cold winter nights, the sky full of stars, a barn owl swooping like a ghost in the silent moonlit farmyard – this isn't true of course, it's just an idea: I have never seen a barn owl in the wild, or if I did I failed to recognise it. But I do remember winter mornings when the ploughed fields are hard frozen beneath a wide, pale blue sky, the ice crisp over the puddles like a properly made crème brûlée.

There was never any attempt at heating in my school dormitory; in winter, in my bed beneath an open window, I lay warm beneath heavy woollen blankets while spots of cold rain fell on my face as I fell asleep, and that felt good. Years later, the memory came back as I sat in a Japanese hot spring in the winter night-time rain.

It is something of a cliché of boarding school memoirs that often you had to break the ice in the wash-basins in the morning; I never did, but I remember that the basins were set in a line in pine boards scrubbed hard for decades so the ridges, the dendronology lines, stood proud like Braille bar codes (driftwood takes me back). The names of the dormitories have always been evocative, names that tie me to my past. In my first house, Stradlings, they were Renaissance scientists: Kepler, Galileo, Tycho and Copernicus, names first known as dormitories before I heard them as scientists; in School House I was at various times in Unicorn, Behemoth and Leviathan; those in 'Gunga Din' were named after Old Boys who had Given Their Lives in the Great War: Frank Sidgwick, Ronnie Poulton, Martin Collier and Charles Fisher (but no mention of my cousin Percy). 'Before the hymn the Skipper would announce the latest names of those who'd lost their lives for King and Country and the Dragon School. Sometimes his gruff old voice was full of tears...'

I might miss English autumns, or, more likely, the idea of an English autumn; being surprised by the early onset of evening, smoke rising vertically from the chimney of the cottage in the valley in the calm as the wind changes, the smell of mushrooms and rotting leaves, a skein of geese overhead like a silk scarf floating in the air.

(Next time I am reincarnated, if I have to be, I would happily settle for being a wild goose, or failing that a sloth; I don't see any advantage in being human. Last time, I was only reincarnated due to a clerical error. I'm not coming back here again – the service has gone off terribly. Not that one should anthropomorphise animals. The lot of most wild animals is one of constant hunger and fear; then again, that has traditionally been the lot of most people; and modern life is little different: nasty, brutish and long.)

Perhaps there is, in England more than elsewhere, a greater likelihood of finding a sword in a stone, an arm reaching out from a pond, something of that sort.

Nostalgia is for things that are only half remembered, or never really known. No one will ever wait for me on the empty platform at Blandford Forum or Mortehoe like the father in the Railway Children beside the willowherb and meadowsweet, and haycocks dry (we're all riding on the Adlestrop express). I seem to remember E Nesbit writing that two other people disembarked from the train that day; the old gentleman was presumably one of them, but who was the third man and what was his unspoken role in the book? Was he the spymaster, pulling the strings unseen except to the most assiduous reader? It might explain the mysterious brief appearance of the Russian revolutionary in the middle of the book. There might be a completely different story going on just below the surface. Was the father actually guilty of treason all along? [No, this isn't true. I have just checked the text and it says 'only three people got out of the 11.54. The first was a countryman with two basketry boxes full of live chickens who stuck their russet heads out anxiously through the wicker bars; the second was Miss Peckitt, the grocer's wife's cousin, with a tin box and three brown-paper parcels; and the third...' The end of an interesting idea.]

Perhaps if I never went back, I would feel I was doing wrong, a probably misplaced sense of duty.

Odysseus lived on Ogygia for seven years and always pined for home, but how soon after his return to Ithaka did he start to wish he was back on the island with Calypso?

And nobody cares about Penelope's suitors; no one stops to think what family obligations, and not of their own choosing, constrained them year after year to stay on Ithaka, one of many competing forlornly for a single, unwilling and probably unwanted prize, a light at the end of the tunnel hardly worth the candle. Surely one of them at least was hoping for Penelope to finish her tapestry or for Odysseus to return, for the deadlock to be broken, so that he too could be free to go off travelling in search of his own Ogygia.

It might make a good short story.

And has anyone thought of writing about the love life, if any, of the minotaur? Every ten years, the Athenians sent seven young women and seven young men as tribute, presumably to do with as he chose. It should have been enough for most people, whatever their tastes, but none of them returned, missing presumed lost; they would have been abusive relationships at best; he was probably too alienated for any kind of empathy, certainly seriously autistic.

And I have often thought Bluebeard a much maligned man. He willingly gave away almost all his life to his wife retaining only a small portion for himself; but even that was too much. In his secret room, the one he had warned her never to enter, she was horrified to find the treasured memories of loves past. She should have known better (but perhaps she too had always felt the need to go into Mr McGregor's garden).

Sometimes you just have to put as much physical distance as possible between yourself and your past; the open road is the only road worth knowing. The compulsion to wander, for a while at least, until it catches up.

Chapter 23

1951–5

One of my strongest memories of the time I lived in High Elms – the first home I really remember, half a mile upriver from Hampton Court Palace and its very English labyrinth – is of going to sleep in my father's office on the second floor, listening to the sound of his typewriter and watching the sky slowly turn a deep shade of blue, royal or possibly even Aegean. From his desk in front of the window, my father would have looked out over the whole length of the garden to the river; he would have seen the heron that perched every evening on the cedar tree half way down the garden, and its mate sitting on top of the weir that cut diagonally across from the far side of the river.

To the right of the cedar was a small rose garden separating the two lawns, both cut in neat stripes. When asked at school what her father did for a living, my older sister Ann, who was then about five, said: 'He cuts the grass and sometimes he writes articles.' When thinking what to write he curled the hair at the side of head with his fingers. Other times he stubbed out cigarettes in a heavy green glass ashtray. I have it still, long unused in the cabinet above my grandfather's desk.

He cut the grass wearing an increasingly tattered Oxford University or Harlequins rugby shirt and, if it was hot, a straw boater. He had been a been a talented schoolboy and university rugby player but in the first five weeks of his second season at the top level he was concussed seven times; his cousin Maurice, who was already a senior specialist at Guy's Hospital, said: 'You do realise you can never play rugby again', and he didn't, a career over before the age of twenty. He might have played for England, and possibly as captain; I never knew how much it mattered. But perhaps concussion was not the only factor; he suffered badly from nerves all his life – not that many people noticed – and he may not have had the temperament for 'the big match'. (Something wrong, an unsound gene in the Mallalieu family; I have it too.)

A year of so after he stopped playing rugby, he was due to make a speech at the Oxford Union alongside Winston Churchill and as they were waiting to enter the chamber Churchill asked: 'Are you nervous?' My father said 'Yes' and he replied: 'So am I, have been before every speech I ever made.' I told this story at dinner with the Russians but I don't know what they made of it. Stalin would have been very different.

Once, instead of cutting straight lines, my father cut Ann's name in the bottom lawn, but when she saw it she ran back crying into the house.

The motor-mower was a pre-war two-stroke Atco painted in green and gold (inexplicably splendid), which my mother had bought at an auction (perhaps the same auction where she bought the sailfish). Ann and I would sometimes curl up in the wheelbarrow and our father would tip the grass cuttings on top of us; I will always remember the combined smell of burnt two-stroke oil and grass cuttings.

Perhaps that was also the auction where she bought a silver, cedarwood-lined cigarette box engraved with initials of Sydney and Beatrice Webb, later stolen along with most of the other silver by the Italian window cleaner. (And I will always remember the combined smell of cedarwood and slightly stale Virginia cigarette tobacco.)

On the far right-hand side of the bottom lawn was a line of weeping willows, where people from the pleasure boats sometimes stopped to pee when they thought no one was looking, and where my mother once found a couple making love. Now, as I discovered much later when walking along the tow path on the far side of the river, there is a high, chain-link fence along the whole length of the garden, which deters intruders but spoils the view.

To the left of the house were garages and greenhouses, beyond them a kitchen garden and eventually a line of copper beeches. The gardener (who wore a brown felt hat and a striped shirt without a collar) once caught an eel in the river and put it in the water tub by the greenhouses. Later that morning, my mother went to dip a tray of bedding plants in the tub and got a rather nasty surprise.

One bonfire night, my father bought fireworks for a party and spent all the money on six very expensive rockets which he let off from a milk bottle on the terrace. (Job's Dairy, the logo embossed in cursive script on the outside of the bottle just below the neck. The Blake illustration to the Book of Job, I Am Old and Ye Are Very Young, always reminds me of that night, the stars in the print echoing the rockets' starburst.) One of the rockets had a broken stick and, instead of going straight up, it flew very fast parallel to the ground about head high, down the lawn as far as the cedar tree, back again and through the doorway to the kitchen courtyard, where it exploded.

I often dream about the house. The form it takes in dreams often bears no resemblance to its physical reality yet it is always immediately recognisable. Sometimes, the river has broken its banks and the water is lapping against the steps of the veranda. Sometimes, there is a small square of wrought-iron railings in the middle of the top lawn with white marble steps leading down to a crypt. Once, part of the house has been converted into a restaurant and I am sitting alone in the deserted dining room wondering if I will ever be served. Occasionally, I am wandering about the house in the middle of the night to the consternation of the current owners. (It is always night, usually the exact real time when I am in bed dreaming.) Once on a cloudless night by the river, I met the gardener who told me to go away as I didn't belong there any more.

In dreams, the house becomes a living, conscious entity, watching the proceedings almost with the expression of a chess player who has just made the winning move and is waiting to see how long it takes you to realise.

The house is not a source of comfort. Perhaps it is a place where something terrible once happened or will one day happen.

It was, certainly at the time I knew it, a very unlucky place. The previous owner had gone bankrupt and it was a year before my parents could get vacant possession; when they moved in the grass on the lawns was waist high, or so I was later told. My father's political career and his personal life both came badly unstuck during the time we lived there.

My mother's parents lived in the flat in the basement. I remember almost nothing of my grandmother Ellen, who was very stylish in a pre-war way with real silk stockings, silver cigarette holder and a regular table at the Ivy restaurant in London; she died of lung cancer shortly after we moved to Hampton Court (far too many Craven A, 'Kinder to your throat' according to the advertisements), much younger than I am now.

She was born working class on Tyneside in the industrial north east of England, and married young; her husband had a good job in the shipyards, volunteered stupidly and was killed on the first day of the Somme, along with all the others. He left her a mother and a widow before she was twenty, one of many without prospects. (When she was dying in great pain she told my mother: 'I keep worrying that if I see him again I might not be able to recognise him; all I remember is that I loved him very much.')

In the early 1920s she met the manager of the local football team (older, richer and married) and they ran off together to the bright lights, which was not the done thing in those days, not at all. Much later when my parents became engaged, one of his sons wrote to my father's eldest brother as 'head of the Mallalieu family' to complain that my mother had been given advantages denied to him and his brother; it didn't go down well, really not at all well. (The general verdict in the wider family was that my father had 'married beneath himself'.)

For thirty years Ellen and my 'step-grandfather' lived a glittering life at the show business end of high society with many talented and entertaining friends. But it all went wrong eventually. When she was dying in hospital Ellen refused to let our mother bring Ann and me to see her: 'I don't want them to remember me as I am now,' she said. Unfortunately, I no longer remember her at all. (I still have a jacket of hers, Astrakhan, unborn lamb, now cut to a waistcoat I have few occasions to wear, but I would have worn it at my wedding reception had I had got back from the pub earlier.)

After she died, my step-grandfather went to the races almost every day, and when he came home he would say he had 'broken even', and eventually he broke even so often that he could no longer meet his debts and the bookmakers sent the heavies round to demand payment.

As well as being what the diarist Paul Johnson later called 'the last true amateur in the Parliamentary Labour Party' (that was probably meant as a compliment), my father wrote parliamentary sketches for Tribune and the New Statesman and sporting essays for the Spectator, forms he pretty much invented or reinvented and are now found in every newspaper. But journalism, even the best, rarely lasts and now his work is almost entirely forgotten. Occasionally in the second-hand bookstalls in Hay-on-Wye, I find old copies of the long-defunct magazine Lilliput with articles he wrote, still as fresh as ever.

Johnson also wrote, in his book Brief Lives, that of all the politicians he had known my father was the only one who was entirely without envy or malice. Looking back, I can see that was probably true and I also know that I cannot honestly say the same about myself.

My father was then at the high tide of his creativity when written words came easily, which was just as well as he was probably not capable of sustained effort at anything other than manual work; but none of his work paid much. It is traditionally the hallmark of a honest politician that he leaves parliament poorer that when he entered; this was certainly true of my father but he overdid it and his debts multiplied as chaotically as the cats that overran the house and garden; at one time we had twenty-four. I remember him trying to drown a litter of kittens in the river, but he was not very good at practical things and he forgot to put a weight in the sack. I remember standing beside him on the bank and sharing his sense of uselessness as we watched the sack float slowly downstream; we heard the kittens crying long after the sack had disappeared into the mist.

Some time later from the garden of the Mitre Hotel, I saw a cat swimming under Hampton Court bridge, but I never imagined it was one of our kittens come of age.

Despite having studied economics at Oxford and Chicago University in the 1930s, my father had very little understanding of money, and he lurched from moments of meanness over trivial sums to extravagance over large amounts. One night at dinner, he asked each of us how much money we had, and when I said 'tenpence' I was told I was the richest member of the family, which was possibly true, but, like most things, the matter was treated lightly and I thought little of it at the time, although the memory stayed.

My father's financial problems took some odd forms. When the old Morris 10 packed up, he borrowed a car for a year or two from the bearded poet Donald Bain; early one winter morning, just as it was getting light, I went into the garage to find an enormous 1935 pillarless Lagonda saloon with running boards and vast silver headlamps, and the smell of old leather and leaking oil has fascinated me ever since. I don't know why. I never wanted to own a car, never learnt to drive and have suffered from car sickness all my life. Perhaps the 'idea' of a car in my head is something fundamentally different from its physical substance. (Perhaps that is true of most of the things I have been interested in.)

I often spent hours climbing round the old Lagonda without touching the ground, but my father never enjoyed driving it. He was troubled by a poisoned hand at the time, and whenever he missed a gear with the pre-synchromesh gate change the pain would shoot up his arm, and the Gilbert and Sullivan songs (Take a Pair of Sparkling Eyes) he habitually sang while driving would be punctuated with shouts of agony. (He was never very good with pain.)

Once, in the garage, I pushed a screwdriver into a power socket to see what would happen, and I can still feel the way my whole body shook: it was like cracking a whip, and the whip retaliating and cracking you.

Whatever my father's financial difficulties, we lived well and there were plenty of parties. At night, I would often be woken by the sound of laughter drifting up from the dining room two floors below. In summer, left-wing and literary figures from Chelsea and Fitzrovia played cricket on the bottom lawn. Michael Foot and his wife, the film director Jill Craigie (she was making a film nearby at Shepperton Studios, The Million Pound Bank Note, with the American actor Gregory Peck), came to dinner and stayed for six months. (Much like

Jenny and me staying with our friend with the beautiful garden.)

My father had been asked to ghost write the autobiography of Charlie Chaplin, at the time one of the most famous people in the world, and we were about to spend the summer in Switzerland with the Chaplins when the project was suddenly shelved, so we never went.

He had been suggested to Chaplin as a possible writer by Jack Hylton, the band leader, impresario and show business friend of my grandmother. (My father had earlier ghost-written a first draft of his 'autobiography' but Hylton had changed his mind about publishing as it inevitably alluded to too many things better left unsaid.)

Chaplin's fame should survive for a couple of centuries at least but Hylton, despite his eminence in his time, is already almost entirely forgotten and is probably best known from the limerick: 'There was a young lady called Gloria/ Who was fucked by Sir Gerald du Maurier,/ Jack Hylton, Jack Payne,/ Sir Gerald again/ And the band of the Waldorf Astoria'. Perhaps in future years this single reference will be all that is known of him, giving him an almost Ozymandias-like significance. He was probably a talented musician as well as a clever businessman and a generous friend but English 1930s 'jazz' band music is surely never due for a revival. I used to know a few enthusiasts, although none under eighty and certainly all now dead. One lunchtime some years back I was having a pint with one of them (name regrettably forgotten), a once famous Tin Pan Alley music agent and Hylton aficionado who in his heyday in the austerity days of the 1950s was a familiar sight driving his enormous American cars through the labyrinthine streets of Soho, and I said in passing: 'Oh I've got something that might interest you', and handed him a copy of the Hylton autobiography. He was very pleased, as you would imagine. Neither he nor any of his friends knew of the manuscript's existence; now, probably, no one cares.

And few people now know or care that the Gloria of the limerick was a real person, a fashion model of the twenties and thirties and briefly famous enough to have a car named after her, the Triumph Gloria (that really is a distinction, if true, although the evidence is inconclusive and it may just be something that people say because it sounds right); she may also have been the model for the milkmaid in the classic Ovaltine poster and just possibly a visual source for Mona Templer in Anthony Powell's A Dance to the Music of Time. Interestingly, for me at any rate, she came from the village in the Pennine hills where my family built their first and all subsequent woollen mills and she could well have been a distant cousin. Her real name was May Kenworthy; when my ancestor Francis was given his land by the son of the Earl of Somewhere he borrowed the money to build his mill from a neighbour called Kenworthy, and church records over the next century and a half often show Mallalieu children marrying Kenworthys. She left school at thirteen to work as a mill girl, perhaps in the Mallalieu mill, but ran off a year later to join the chorus line, when May became Gloria and she never looked back except to write her memoirs for the News of the World (or more likely have them ghost written).

Gloria and my father were near contemporaries and their paths should have crossed either in the village or later in London, if only as mutual friends of Jack Hylton, although I never remember him mentioning her name. Possibly with good reason.

I don't think anyone remembers Jack Payne for any reason at all.

To modern ears the limerick sounds a little uncharitable ('What is the definition of a slut?' says my Greek Rasta friend Panos. 'A woman who will fuck anyone except you.') The lawyer and writer John Mortimer, who was a lifetime friend and career colleague of my sister's (in his Rumpole stories she became 'the Portia of our Chambers'), wrote the screenplay for the television adaption of John Fowles' The Ebony Tower and had the drunken artist, played by Laurence Olivier, recite the limerick after dinner and adding 'I have always had the greatest respect for Gloria.' As one should.

The room below my father's office housed a billiard table and, in the corner to the left of the fireplace, a dumb waiter to the kitchen in the basement. My mother said you could put the dirty plates in it after a dinner party and wind it half way down so that you didn't have to see the mess first thing in the morning. I always wanted to sit in it and be wound down to the kitchen, but I never did, and certainly won't ever do so now. (I also always wanted to go to an English beach armed with proper spades and a wheelbarrow and at low tide build an enormous sandcastle that had a chance of surviving against the incoming sea for at least an hour or two. But I won't now, either.)

After losing a game of billiards, the charismatic Welsh politician Nye Bevan complained that the table was too low, so the following week some men came from Burroughs & Watts in Soho Square to raise it up on blocks. My parents didn't approve of war toys, but Nye said: 'Every boy should have a gun', and the next weekend he brought me a double-barrelled shotgun, which fired real corks (attached to the barrels with string so they couldn't do any damage).

Men in suits and ties from Harrods (or more likely men from Harrods in suits and ties) came to polish the parquet floor in the hall with sheepskin mufflers attached to their knees.

A door at the end opened onto the stairs to the kitchens and at the bottom of the flight were boxes of porcelain fuses often attended to by a local handyman called Julius Caesar (that was what he said and I knew no reason to doubt him); his clothes and the way he talked (schmutter and patter) were, I can see now, based on the comedian Max Miller. He once took our nanny out for the evening but she said she wasn't going again because he was 'all hands'. (She later married a soldier called Fred, who has always been a hero of mine.)

The kitchens were two gloomy rooms smelling of burnt toast, which we fed to the pet rabbits in the kitchen garden, and gas, which leaked from the enormous black range. One of the cats had kittens on the kitchen floor, much to the horror of Michael Foot who had just come down for breakfast. (Another had kittens in one of the drawers of my father's desk, the desk that later went to my sister's chambers in the Temple; it is probably still there – the desk not the cat.) It was while my father and Michael were eating breakfast that the heavies from William Hill came round to dun my grandfather, but they went away empty handed, disconcerted to be confronted by two MPs or, more probably, two friends of Lord Beaverbrook, the most powerful British press baron of the age: his newspapers were 'robustly' right-wing but he had a curious fondness for young and talented left-wing journalists.

Out of sight from the window in my father's study was a path that snaked its way through the shrubs and trees to the right of the top lawn. Half way along the path was an air-raid shelter where my mother kept chickens and where the gardener once caught a rat. It was caught alive in a 'humane trap', a galvanised wire cage with a door that opened inwards but not out, posing a problem of how to dispose of the contents. The rat was enormous and not afraid of anything, and it stared through the bars with a look of defiance. The largest of the tom cats was brought, but on seeing the rat it walked slowly backwards, never taking its eyes off the cage until it was at a safe distance to turn and run. Then the gardener brought a tin bath and began to fill it with water, whereupon the rat lost its bravado and began to scream.

The weir on the far bank of the river looked like a flight of steps covered in deep green weed, and the water flowed over them so evenly that it looked like glass. Only at the bottom step, where the water reached the river, was there any sense of movement. To a child who couldn't swim, they were fascinating: it seemed impossible to walk down the steps without slipping to certain death in the deep water.

For a time, a converted motor torpedo boat belonging to a Mr Saunders (Saunders of the river) was moored beside the landing stage beyond the copper beeches. One winter morning, when the dew was so heavy on the grass that you could see your footprints stretching away across the lawn, I went down to the river on my own and saw Mr Saunders lying on the landing stage as though he was asleep. I sat on the steps looking at him until he said: 'Please go and get your parents,' and later an ambulance took him away.

Thirty years later, I was in a pub in Esher in Surrey and the landlord said: 'There's a man called Saunders looking for you. He'll be in shortly. He said he used to live at the bottom of your garden.' But he never showed up, and I didn't expect him to: High Elms is a place of enchantment into which the present cannot enter. It is as though it exists only in dreams, and on the few occasions when I have seen the physical building since I left, the effect has been as shocking as if I had seen an Alien.

The other night, I dreamed I was in the dining room looking out towards the river. The sky turned wild, and black clouds swirled like ink poured into water. I saw a wave coming fast upstream, and suddenly the entire house was underwater; the glass in the window stretched and bowed absurdly inwards but somehow didn't break. The water subsided but the structural integrity of the building had been destroyed, and it trembled dangerously with every step I took.

Perhaps the reason why I was sleeping in my father's office was because I was afraid to sleep in my own room.

My room was on the top floor under the eaves. Above my bed was a small inlaid wooden picture, long ago lost, of a circus with an elephant balancing on a ball in the foreground. Ann and I used to sit on the bed in pyjamas and dressing gowns while our father read aloud from Moonfleet (the undertow) or Treasure Island (the black spot), or poems by Walter de la Mare (in the twilight drenched with dew).

The room had built-in cupboards about three feet high along the sloping side walls. If you crawled along a cupboard into the darkness, right at the end you found some more doors leading into further storage space deeper under the eaves. This had been forgotten by the previous owners, and when they moved out they left behind various objects which I later retrieved from the darkness. They included, among other things now forgotten, some wartime gas masks and a box that my mother took away when I showed it to her. Many years later, I learned it was someone's ashes. (My grandmother had collected Lalique glassware in the twenties and thirties, but by the time she died it was badly out of fashion – for ever as most people would have assumed – so her collection was wrapped up, put away and forgotten about, perhaps even in the same cupboards under the eaves; much later, in the sixties, long after we had moved away, when I had begun to discover the joys of arts nouveau, deco and moderne, I mentioned Lalique to my mother and she said: 'I wonder what happened to it.')

But the oddest thing about the room was the holes in the wall. They were about a third of an inch in diameter and three quarters of an inch deep, drilled or punched into the plaster, and I would often wake up in the morning to find another one or two had appeared. Like most things in the family, this was treated as a joke, but my mother took it seriously enough to go and speak to whatever was causing it, saying something along the lines of 'I don't know who you are or what you're doing here, and we don't mind you being here, but we have small children in the house and if you upset them we'll have to call in a priest and have you exorcised'. It was, perhaps, an unorthodox way to talk to a poltergeist, but from then on there were no more holes. But I continued for a long time to be uneasy about sleeping in the room.

My parents sold High Elms when I was eight and bought a smaller house in the country near Oxford. (It was also haunted; some things you can't easily shrug off or escape from just by moving away.) The headmaster of my school in Teddington told my parents I was the cleverest boy he had ever taught, and later, when Ann began to make a name for herself, one of my old teachers wrote to my mother to congratulate her, adding: 'What has happened to Ben? I always thought he would go far.' Which perhaps I did, although not in many directions that were ultimately worth exploring.

A few years ago, I was waiting at the doctor's to collect my prescription; leafing through the magazines, I saw an estate agent's advertisement for High Elms. 'A charming early Victorian house,' it said, and I started laughing, causing the other people in the waiting room to look up and think about edging away. My father had charm, perhaps more than was good for him, but the house was very different. I rang the estate agents and asked them to send me a brochure, but they never did.

The last time I saw High Elms was in odd circumstances. One New Year's Day, Jenny and I loaded our children into the back of our campervan at four in the morning and set off to stay with some friends in Bere Alston in Devon. The roads were deserted and, unusually for London, the houses and gardens were covered in deep snow. The clutch began to play up going through Kingston (I don't know why we were going that way), and when we reached The Green it packed up completely. We turned round just past High Elms, which loomed wide awake out of the darkness, and we limped back home in second gear.

Chapter 24

1954

My father and I often spent afternoons together watching rugby, cricket or football. Once in the bar at Lords cricket ground, he introduced me to the great pre-war batsman Patsy Hendren, but all I remembered later was his hands, which were large and shiny.

Later, also at Lords, I shook hands with a gentle, sad-faced giant with the splendid name of Boris Karloff, with no explanation of whom he might have been, and was disconcerted to find that he had Patsy Hendren's hands. (Is this true, or a later exaggeration, just something that sounds good? Once you write them down, memories, however dubious, become fixed. But one of the advantages of growing older is that there are fewer people around to dispute your version of the past.)

I have often maintained that Karloff based his interpretation of Frankenstein's monster on the English cricketer Ted Alletson. I don't have any evidence for this; it is just another idea that sounds right and should be right, too good to be ignored. I have a photograph of Alletson (in storage), a giant, simultaneously both awkward and graceful as giants often are, a doomed Goliath; his face is blurred (this may just have been because he moved unintentionally when asked not to, but it gives him a spiritually drained 'post-possession' look, as though something has been withheld, not for reproduction; perhaps also something of the look of a blind minotaur).

One afternoon in Brighton in 1911, he played the most extraordinary innings in the history of cricket, possibly the single most extraordinary performance in all sport, and he never did anything remotely similar before or since. It is hard to know why he was playing at all; no one considered him much of a batsman and no one other than himself rated his bowling – he hadn't been allowed to bowl at all in the Sussex innings and when Nottinghamshire batted he didn't go in until the fall of the sixth wicket, far down among the tail-enders. His team were pleasantly surprised with his performance before lunch, impressive if not particularly unusual, scoring forty-seven runs in fifty minutes. After lunch, he took another ten minutes to reach fifty; and then he passed out of the known world. His second fifty took only fifteen minutes and in the following fourteen he hit a further eighty-nine runs. His scoring would have been even faster had play not been suspended for five minutes while the ball was prised out from between the timbers of the pavilion where it had become jammed (or so my father said), and the umpire eventually gave him out even though the fielder who took the catch insisted he was over the boundary at the time. People later suggested that Alletson was hitting the ball so hard that the umpires became fearful of their physical safety, but it is more likely they realised they were witnessing something that was in danger of transgressing the normally accepted rules of nature, overstepping the boundaries; they had become fearful of their psychic safety.

That was the only century or any performance of note in his brief career, or in his long life, Many years later, my father and his friend and fellow cricket writer Alan Gibson found Alletson as an old man still working in a very modest capacity as a groundsman in Nottinghamshire. He apologised for being the cause of a wasted journey but he had nothing to tell them about his innings because he had never been able to remember anything about it.

Chapter 25

1954

My parents had bought High Elms as another compromise, hoping it might be a country house within easy reach of London, and at first sight the area still looks rural: the house is immediately across the road from The Green, and beyond that is Bushey Park with as good a collection of ancient oak trees as you could find anywhere. But it was really a no man's land, neither town nor country and the road between the house and the Green was a dangerous place. The bus stop was directly opposite on the other side of the road, but Ann and I were told always to get off at the Palace, cross at the zebra crossing and walk back down. Once, Ann was knocked over at the crossing by a taxi. The driver brought her home and rang the bell, pausing only to say she had 'fallen down' before disappearing fast. She looked dazed; he looked shifty – even to a five year old like me, already beginning to wander off, making my first tentative steps towards the ultra-violet end of the spectrum. (Children's shoes have far to go.)

I was also once hit by a car on the same road, further along towards Hampton, but that was certainly not the driver's fault. I thought I saw Ann and my grandfather on the other side of the road and ran out without looking, colliding with the passenger door of a swerving green car, the inevitable accident on the familiar journey.

The vicar of Hampton [or possibly the rector of St Mary's Teddington], who was passing at the time, gave me an aspirin which I bit into by mistake, and I still remember the taste.

The road outside High Elms was strung with a network of overhead wires to power the double-deckered electric trolley buses, as streamlined and futuristic as anything in the comic strip Dan Dare, Pilot of the Future, more 'modern' than anything on the roads today, a promise of things to come that somehow failed to materialise.

Sometimes the metal arms on the roof of the bus fell off the overhead wires and the conductor had to get out and re-attach them with a long wooden boat hook, a very low-tech solution to the problem, although it didn't seem incongruous at the time, perhaps due to the road's, albeit brief, proximity to the river.

The connection where the trolley bus arms touched the wires flashed in the fog. Those were the last days before the Clean Air Act when the London smogs were at their worst. Some mornings, you could see clearly for about fifteen feet then beyond that was a wall of white, sometimes yellow, almost like a cavern carved out of deep snow. One winter afternoon, it got dark at two o'clock.

Every morning from the age of six, I took the 304 trolley bus on my own to my school in Teddington, buying a tuppenny-halfpenny-half-fare ticket.

I no longer remember what the next-door building on the left-hand side of High Elms really looked like (and it isn't there any more), but in the dream landscape it is a large wooden boathouse, almost identical to a police barracks I used to know in the middle of Istanbul, up the hill from Topkapi and round the corner from the Pudding Shop. Whenever I was in Istanbul I would usually go to see it because of its association with the dream house, but one year I found it had disappeared and been replaced by an anonymous concrete building that looked as though it had been standing there for years. Do we really dream repeatedly of the same imaginary places, or do we do so only once, the dream implanting a series of false memories of earlier dreams?

Beyond the 'boathouse', a line of small suburban villas stretched towards what had once been the village of Hampton; most of them, for some reason, had 'To Let' signs by the gates, rarely 'For Sale'. At some point, the bus route passed a Palladian folly by the river. (In the dream landscape, this has grown into a much larger structure and is always on the other side of the road in Bushey Park, perhaps on sounder ground.)

To the right of High Elms, the road led directly to the palace gates.

Five doors down was St Anne's, owned by a stockbroking family called Wright of archetypal Englishness like the Wilcoxes in Howards End and of such solidity and self-assurance that it is almost inconceivable that they are not still living there unchanged in a time warp, eating Weetabix for breakfast spread with butter and Oxford marmalade, the younger sons doing noisy impressions of Roy Salvadori in a BRM, and the Caran d'Ache drawing of Toscanini [or perhaps Paderewski?] still hanging in the hall. The house was stockbroker Tudor with alpine and possibly Arts and Crafts influences, the kind of house Rupert Bear lived in, and maybe William Brown, the kind of house that until recently would be regarded as architecturally worthless, but very expensive.

Beyond St Anne's was the Carleton Hotel with a sign at the front that always said: 'Luncheon 1pm'. (Does it still?) Later came the Cardinal Wolsey pub; children were not allowed inside, but in early morning the landlord opened the doors to allow the newly scrubbed pine floor to dry, and the timeless smell of wet wood and stale beer reached out to me on the pavement as I walked by. The smell of beer has not changed. But once as a child I swallowed a mouthful of cider and the taste, which I still remember intensely, had no similarity with anything I now recognise as cider. It is not simply that I now like something that once seemed strange and unpleasant; my perception of the taste itself is now dramatically different, just as if something that once looked green now registers in my brain as red. (If I take a mouthful of cider and suddenly try to force it up to the top of my mouth and the back of my nose, there is a faint echo of the remembered taste, but only very faint.)

Beyond the Cardinal Wolsey the road passed – at least in the dream landscape – the 'grace and favour apartments', cold grey buildings mostly inhabited by impoverished members of deposed European royal families. I never saw any of the inhabitants, or if I did so I failed to recognise them without their crowns; I much later imagined them walled up in their rooms like Tibetan lamas. Occasionally, they lowered wicker baskets on ropes from their windows and the fishmonger would place a single herring inside, or so I was told (or later imagined being told).

A peculiarity of the road, or possibly of my memory of it, was the unusual number of bizarre invalid carriages, even older than their occupants. They were all painted black and shared the same basic design: a small single wheel at the front, a more conventional wheelchair at the back but with the seat set closer to the ground, the occupant's legs stretched out in front wrapped in a sombre tweed (perhaps Black Watch) blanket or in some kind of dark waterproof webbing like a bat's wing. Very like the cloak (or mantle?) Burne-Jones put over the king's legs in The Sleep of Arthur in Avalon. The means of propulsion was invariably peculiar: sometimes a tiny petrol engine, pre-first world war, perched above the front wheel, driving it by chain, the entire mechanism steered by a very long pair of handlebars; sometimes, almost unbelievably, the contraption was propelled manually, a chain running from the front wheel to a single handlebar from where it was wound by hand. (What is the manual equivalent of pedals? Handals?)

The encounter that remains most strongly in my memory took place as I was walking up towards the palace early one morning under a low mantle of black cloud threatening heavy rain, a narrow band of sunlight dazzling at the edges. Coming towards me was an invalid carriage propelled by two levers on either side of the seat – the occupant pushed one forward and pulled the other back, proceeding slowly in a series of jerks. I could later never decide how the power was transmitted to the wheels, perhaps a kind of ratchet mechanism like the hand-and-lever-powered railway carts in silent films.

It was certainly hard work for the driver, his sinews strained like bone, veins throbbing on his face. Never before, or since, had I seen anyone concentrate so hard on anything, his clear china-blue eyes sightless to everything except the road ahead, if that. He passed by very slowly, two miles an hour at most, no more than three feet away.

I remember the old man's skin as dry as paper, like that of an Egyptian mummy, his white hair hovering in a single layer half an inch above his head.

Two trains passing in opposite directions.

Chapter 26

1952

'Erif Der was sitting on a bank of shingle and throwing pebbles into the Black Sea; for a girl she threw very straight. She was thinking a little about magic but mostly about nothing at all.'

I can tell from the first page that the author can write well. But the prospect of seven hundred more pages is not a comfortable one. A didactic mixture of Fabian socialism, Oxford classicism and The Golden Bough weighs heavily on twenty-first century sensibilities.

I am sitting on Carradale beach trying to read The Corn King and The Spring Queen. Once, it was widely regarded as a classic of modern English literature but now it is almost entirely forgotten; as I sit on the shingle, there might be no other person in the world with this book open in front of them. There ought to be some criteria to explain why some things last and some don't, why in fifty years time Geoff Dyer will have disappeared while Toby Litt will be boring generations of A-level students with his set books. Or vice versa. [Probably both forgotten along with the rest of us.] Why, at Pooh sticks, some twigs are carried far away on the stream while others come to nothing among the stones.

Behind the beach, rising above the trees are the turrets of Carradale House, where the book's author, Naomi Mitchison, lived for most of her adult life and where as a very small child I and my family spent a summer.

Every summer, Naomi and her husband Dick kept open house for some twenty or thirty adult guests and a dozen or more children who were allowed to run wild. In the summer of 1952, I was the youngest, definitely at the bottom of the pecking list.

Naomi was the laird in the big house. It is now almost impossible to imagine what a shock that must have been to such a small, tight society as Carradale: tight as in tightly knit, uptight and, for most of the men, given any excuse to escape responsibility, drunk. In the days before television, remote communities were seriously remote. This was a time when women were not allowed in the public bars of most Highland pubs. Naomi believed in feminism, open marriage, nude bathing and socialism, but she fought the corner of the local community better than anyone before or since.

One night on the back seat of the last bus from Tarbert, she spent the journey kissing one of the local fishermen. The bus was dark but all the other passengers would have been starkly aware of what was going on. And before noon the next day, so would the whole village. She wrote a nice poem about being a fishing boat out at sea and coming alongside her lover's boat (a different lover from the one on the bus): '… and sometimes your face is above me/and sometimes below.'

When I first stayed at Carradale, she and the other adults went out at night with the local poacher to poach her own salmon.

Carradale bay is over a mile long, warmed by the Gulf Stream and protected on all sides from the worst of the weather. Trees grow tall, rhododendrons are rampant and the gunnera, like radioactive rhubarb, is as much at home as in Cornwall's Roseland peninsula. Revisiting as an adult many years later, I found that Carradale days were just as I had remembered them, starting grey, the mist rolling in, very low and damp, from the hills, then often turning into beautiful, bright evenings until the sun set somewhat prematurely below the saddle of the hills.

As I sit on the shingle, the beach is almost entirely empty, a few people walking their dogs, no one swimming. At one end, largely hidden among the ponticum, gorse and bracken is a small camp site where my family and I are staying. It rains most nights, but there are few better sensations than lying warm and comfortable in a tent with someone you love listening to the rain on the flysheet (so long as you are confident that it isn't going to leak). When it isn't raining, we can hear the sea.

The beach is where the river Carra meets the sea: the water is black and peaty and terribly cold. At the tideline, I find oak and hawthorn leaves among the seaweed, which seems unnatural, almost magical. Very Erif Der.

Sixty years ago, the Mallalieus went swimming every day to the amusement of the rest of the house party who would wrap up in woollens and come down to the beach to watch. The later generation of Mallalieus are not so hardy.

For some reason, my parents never took us back to Carradale. Naomi had a talent for friendship, and I was sorry not to have known her as an adult. I would have liked her to have met Jenny and the children, turning up unexpected on a rainy winter night and being made welcome, a still point in a changing world.

The once fabulous wealth melted away, and for the last thirty years of her life the house and garden slowly unravelled around her, which somehow seems much as it should be, a natural process. I had not realised how much my taste in gardens owed to Carradale.

The outside of the house with its beautiful windows looks much as I remembered it. (At the age of five I had been very impressed to find a turret room converted into a loo, one of the few rooms I recognise when the new owner shows me round.)

The annual summer parties were, perhaps, a gathering of the British upper middle class intelligentsia, then a surprisingly small group of often interconnected families which dominated the intellectual and cultural life of Britain for over a century and has now effectively disappeared, like a village subsumed into the outskirts of a town. They were, for the most part, families who after making large amounts of money in the industrial revolution had relocated to Oxford, Cambridge or London and devoted their energies to the arts, sciences and radical causes, in which they were immensely successful, although none of their efforts did much to restock their family coffers.

There are still people who share their values (probably more than ever) but they don't have the money, and they lack the assurance. It is unlikely that Naomi or any of the adults I remember from years ago ever thought they might be wrong. Revisiting the house and its grand but now empty wine cellars, I feel like Matthew Arnold on Dover beach: 'The Sea of Faith/ Was once, too, at the full, and round earth's shore/ Lay like the folds of a bright girdle furled./ But now I only hear/ Its melancholy, long, withdrawing roar.'

The intellectual middle classes had an arrogance no less than that of the commercial bourgeoisie, although very different. The latter despised the poor, regarding them almost as a different race, but they were only fooling themselves, trying to pull up the drawbridge behind them, desperate to put as much distance as possible between themselves and their roots; and occasionally while awake in the night with financial worries they knew that the only thing that really separated them from the poor was money – without it they would be in every way ruined. They kept good care of their money, guarding it carefully from anyone who threatened to take it away from them. The intellectual middle classes, on the other hand, believed in 'the equality of man', making a conscious point of despising no one (except the commercial bourgeoisie from whom they themselves were, of course, descended), but they also believed in the supreme importance of education and intellect, particularly their own; as a result, they were careless with money, often contemptuously so, with inevitable consequences.

Intelligence has much to be said for it, quite rightly, but it is not a guarantee or even a prerequisite of success. Unintelligent people are usually underestimated as rivals until it is too late: Stalin's rise through the Russian Communist Party is a classic case – the middle-class intellectuals were delighted to have an uneducated peasant on their side and, probably more important, to be seen to be promoting his cause, but when they next looked up he was smirking down at them from the balcony at their show trials.

One of the cleverer Mitchison grandchildren (they were all clever) told Ann and me a story, which I never doubted for several years, that nearby there was a grove of trees on a small hill and in the middle was an entrance to a cave full of gold, but the further you went inside the more you lost the will to return to the surface and you stayed there until you starved to death. Sixty years ago, as we set out on our journey home, I thought I saw the grove of trees through the car window. Ann was older and more sceptical. This time, on my way home, I look out to see if it is still there, but I fail to find it.

Chapter 27

1953

The only present my godfather John Macadam ever gave me was a pewter tankard, which was not an obvious choice of gift for a five year old and clearly not a lot of thought or expense had gone into its selection: a badge on the front said 'Presented by the Racing Pigeon Association' and at some point in its history it had been sat on so that it didn't sit straight and tended to fall over when full of liquid.

I looked for it when we were packing up the London house but I couldn't find it; it should have been at the back of the glass cabinet that sat on top of my grandfather's desk, but it wasn't there any more.

I don't remember John Macadam well as he died not long after he gave me the tankard, but one summer, the year after we went to Carradale, we spent a holiday in the Devon fishing village of Brixham where he had a house called Hangover Cottage, Temperance Steps, which rose unsteadily from the harbour. (Years later when I went to the Aegean island of Hydra I couldn't work out where it reminded me of, and then suddenly I realised.) The ground floor had a small courtyard at the front, home to an impressive collection of enormous snails [or possibly slugs], and the top floor was a single, large attic room, John's office, with a desk, bookshelves all round and a tiger rug on the floor so that when you climbed the stairs you were suddenly confronted by it face to face; at the far end of the room, French windows opened onto a small walled garden whose only memorable feature was a wooden pole with an electricity transformer. Once when John failed to pay his bill, the electricity board cut off his supply, so he borrowed an axe from the local pub and cut down their pole.

He usually lived beyond his means, spending even more on paintings than he did on whisky. When broke, as he often was, he gave his pictures away to stop his creditors taking them, although sadly all he gave me was the tankard, which his creditors wouldn't have wanted. There was, it was said, a full-length, life-sized portrait by Graham Sutherland which John gave to the Press Club where it stayed for many years 'looking longingly towards the bar'. I often wondered what happened to it after the Press Club closed.

And John Macadam himself has disappeared, almost without trace. He wrote journalism that bordered on literature; he also wrote plays and at least one novel, but none of it has lasted. He may have been one of the better known writers of his day but in the lottery of lasting fame he drew a blank. A trawl of the internet found so little that I thought I might be spelling the name wrong, but 'John McAdam' and 'John Macadem' were equally fruitless. (Can a trawl produce fruit? Perhaps it should be 'fishless'.)

Nor could I find any mention of Temperance Steps in Brixham although I did eventually unearth a house for sale called Amethyst Cottage, Temperance Place, almost certainly the same house if smaller than I remembered it, as most things usually are. (The estate agent called it 'deceptively spacious' as you would expect.) It is unlikely to have a blue plaque on the front wall or if anyone knows or cares about its history.

Then last Christmas in Hay-on-Wye, upstairs in Addyman's bookshop (Hey Mr Addy Man, addy me banana!), I found a copy of The Macadam Road by John Macadam, published, probably posthumously, by The Sportsman's Book Club in 1957. It is nominally an autobiography, but journalists of John's day were reticent about writing about themselves. His wife, who died very young and was said to have been a great beauty, is not mentioned; the American writer Elizabeth Keen, whom he once lived with, is referred to only briefly in connection with a play they collaborated on. 'She is now perched on a mountain-top in the US West and has no part in this present writing,' is all he says. The Macadam Road is more a memoir of largely forgotten sporting and entertainment heroes of the twenties, thirties and forties.

It isn't a book that is likely to be 'rediscovered'.

It is probably fair to say that he wrote fluently but too prolifically and usually too close to deadline. His style is a welcome reaction against the pompous formality of the preceding generation (sports journalists really did once write about 'tapping the claret' and 'suspending the spheroid in the rigging') but his colloquialisms, 'by golly!', have dated badly. Often though there are intimations that he could in other circumstances have written a much better book, not least in a quietly lyrical description of taking his boat out of Brixham harbour in the autumn twilight and wondering what he should really be writing about; someone should put it in an anthology, but probably won't.

The book's pictures also belong to a different age. The great Alex James in his last match in an Arsenal shirt looks as unlike a modern footballer as it is possible to be, although probably none the worse for that. And what would modern audiences make of 'Two great Glasgow drolls: Tommy Lorne and Tommy Morgan'? Humour rarely lasts long. I liked the pictures of John playing a ukelele – something I had forgotten – and of John chatting with fishermen on the quay at Brixham. The biggest shock in the book is the photograph captioned: 'James Proudfoot, well-known painter, in his Chelsea studio with the greatly discussed portrait of the author he painted in 1953', the picture wrongly attributed to Sutherland.

It is an unusual photograph, the kind that Bill Brandt might have taken (and possibly did, but unattributed), full of strange diagonals. The first thing you notice is the painting in the foreground, the painter himself only later emerging from the shadows, which makes his determined and rather knowing stare all the more unsettling.

Proudfoot is playing, for all it's worth, the role of the archetypal Chelsea artist of the fifties, complete with beard, smock and pipe; he leans against the canvas in a studied bohemian manner, the angle of his head mimicking that of the portrait; he almost appears to be communicating directly with you in the present as though there is a truth immediately obvious to both you and him that eluded most of his contemporaries.

Proudfoot is no longer a well-known painter although on the

evidence of this one picture he probably deserves to be. It is easy to see why it might have been mistaken for Sutherland but there is also something of Egon Schiele about it, possibly even Basil Hallward.

The person in the painting is someone nearing the end of his life having spent far too long on a diet of too many cigarettes, too much Scotch whisky and not enough food, a sad mouth hiding beneath the false gaiety of a handlebar moustache. And as for staring longingly towards the bar, it is more a case of sitting on the railway tracks and staring blankly at the oncoming train.

Chapter 28

1954

A few years back, I was staying with friends in Bere Alston, one of those slightly odd small towns on the edge of Dartmoor, and had gone to buy a morning paper when I unexpectedly had he sensation that I had been there before, although I couldn't remember when and nothing looked familiar. The sensation was strongest outside a small, entirely undistinguished nonconformist chapel, and I suddenly realised that this was where at the age of at six or seven I had heard my father's old friend Alan Gibson preach a sermon; I had probably not thought of him for years.

The chapel was locked and I couldn't go in, but it was unlikely to have changed much in the intervening half century: a small bare room with two banks of high-backed, dark-stained wooden pews, the walls plain whitewashed plaster, no heating, definitely no pictures. Alan towered above us from his dark wooden pulpit, a tall, thin man with large bones, powerful eyes and a shock of very black hair shortly to become prematurely white.

'Why is he angry?' I whispered to my mother; he wasn't usually like that. 'Shh,' she said.

As an art form, the fire-and-brimstone sermon has gone out of fashion, hardly done at all and never by anyone who is likely do it well – a warning of imminent damnation inspired as much by the beauty of words as by the glory of God (possibly much the same thing).

Afterwards Alan was his old self, my father – always lavish with charm and praise – complimenting him on his performance.

In his old self, Alan was much like my father, a flawed romantic more concerned with the beautiful idea than the small print. They were both talented, affable, unreliable men, with no sense of thrift and a tendency to wander, but bigger people than those you find nowadays, or so it seems to me looking back.

Alan wrote, mostly about cricket, for The Times, and he was a Radio Three Test Match Special regular with John Arlott, EW Swanton and Brian Johnstone; on a good day he was much the best of the four, erudite and literate and with a beautiful speaking voice, although becoming more eccentric as the shadows lengthened. That was in the days when it didn't seem odd to have cricket commentary on the BBC radio Third Programme, alongside the classical music, much like bullfights are still reported on the Spanish arts pages. My parents' old friend Neville Cardus was the Guardian's cricket correspondent in summer and music correspondent in winter. The two are not entirely dissimilar disciplines: in music, the sound of a note means nothing without the memory of the previous note and the anticipation of the one to come; in cricket, the duel between a bowler and a batsman follows a similar pattern (it's no good watching the edited highlights). In his cricket reports Cardus often compared cricket to music but he never compared music to cricket in his music reviews; but whatever he wrote about music is forgotten: he is only remembered as a cricket writer.

One of the many puzzling things about modern journalism is that while the newspaper space allocated to sport has increased enormously, less and less of it is actually worth reading. Perhaps the time when Alan and my father were writing was briefly a golden age, a more leisurely, more generous time when sports writers had the freedom to go off piste, particularly when writing about cricket – you could spend all day, much of in the bar, writing and polishing a few hundred words, and often the less play there was the better the report would be. My father was once invited to Bradfield School to write about a promising schoolboy batsman called Ted Dexter; the match was abandoned due to rain (I remember the day well) but my father undeterred wrote instead about how when he was a boy he had sat in the rain immediately behind the former prime minister Herbert Asquith at the school's outdoor Greek theatre and had been impressed by how he had taken off his hat to shelter his copy of the text of the play they was watching. (How many recent prime ministers have been capable of following a Greek text? Asquith was probably the last, although Gladstone would have been even more fluent and might not have needed a text in front of him.) Alan would sometimes write more about the barmaid at the Bristol cricket ground or train failures at Didcot station than about the game in question, a licence no longer permitted. Perhaps it's an illusion and a good writer just appears to have all the time in the world, like a good batsman.

On the day I heard Alan preach, we were staying in the Gibsons' comfortable, untidy house in Devon because Alan and my father had been invited to play in the benefit match for Johnny Lawrence, Somerset's soon-to-retire Yorkshire-born leg-spinner – leg spin was an under-appreciated skill, particularly in Yorkshire where it was regarded as somewhat heretical (and, worse, wasteful), which was why he had to earn his living in Somerset. He was an old-fashioned professional cricketer, never giving less than his best but always overlooked for the England team, underpaid even by the standards of the day and now forgotten outside the pages of Wisden where the bare statistics of his career give little indication of his skill; but he was a true artist in the quiet way the English occasionally do well.

The benefit match was unfortunately a washout, and it rained for much of the holiday although Alan's hospitality always cheered it up. Fine or not, we went most days to the beach – Hope Cove or Bigbury-on-Sea, where the children raced across the sands and Alan pretended that the echo from the far side of the estuary was someone shouting back, and I was just young enough to be uncertain whether he was joking. At breakfast Alan said: 'A good post: two cheques and no bills', a sentiment echoed by freelance writers down the ages. When the grown ups went out for the evening, we children were babysat by a very large lady called Mrs Morris, but when Alan came to drive her home, he had difficulty finding the gear lever, or so he said later with much enjoyment.

Perhaps Alan was then at the high tide of his life, before high spirits and comradeship deflated into alcoholism. He was, it was said later, troubled by a sense of having wasted his life: he was awarded a first at Oxford without apparently ever attending a lecture, was President of the Union (like my father a decade or so before) and could talk as fluently about Hazlitt and the Romantic poets as about cricket; he should have achieved more, although, possibly, lasting achievement should be regarded as a bonus rather than a prerequisite of a good life. And he felt guilty about his drinking and his failure as a husband and father, which, of course, only makes things worse.

He was dropped by Test Match Special in 1975; not turning up for a live broadcast is never a good move, and sometimes when he did turn up it was an even bigger mistake. Musing out loud on the name of a New Zealand batsman, he is supposed to have said: 'Cunis, an unusual name, neither one thing nor the other!' TMS was a lot duller after he went.

Demons and despair got the better of him, but not without a fight. He had spells in mental hospitals and his last years were spent in a nursing home.

Looking back years later, I expected to find that Alan was almost entirely forgotten like most of the talented people I knew in my childhood, but it was a delight to discover how generous Alan's obituaries had been, even those written by people who cannot have known him at his best; and although his books are out of print they can still be found second hand on the internet. His son Anthony has published a collection of his best journalism, and there might even be some tapes of his cricket commentaries somewhere; but there won't be any recordings of his fire-and-brimstone sermons.

Chapter 29

1956

One dark January night when I was eight years old, my old life came to an end when my parents took me to my new school for the first time and left me at the boarding house.

The housemaster had a horribly false jollity, full of menace like a Punch and Judy man, ringing his hands with Dickensian unctuousness, especially friendly to my father whom he obviously wanted to impress (although few people's attitude to my father was entirely unequivocal: as a libertarian socialist he had broken ranks – even though his principles were essentially only those of the idealised prep school prefect, which, indeed, he had been: he believed that everyone had something useful to contribute and deserved to be listened to, treated with respect and given their fair share of the rewards; most of all, he had a hatred of bullying – and there was always something suspect about the Mallalieu family, even more skeletons than cupboards) but I didn't like him and I could tell immediately that he didn't like me: he despised boys who were afraid, although he probably enjoyed exercising power over them. I tried to make a joke but it wasn't funny and no one laughed.

The house was the most desperate place I have ever been to. Abandon hope. It has haunted me ever since, the smaller details, forgotten or repressed, haunting subliminally, years later provoking life-altering decisions I never understood.

My father had loved the school; his time there was not just the best days of his life but its highest point (from then on downwards, slowly at first, faster later on – downhill all the way really): head boy inevitably, colours in all the sports, winner of the speech prize three years running, lead roles in all the annual Shakespeare plays and Gilbert and Sullivan operas; in Summoned by Bells, John Betjeman, his school contemporary and eventual poet laureate, famously described him as 'the perfect boy'. It was an impossible standard to live up to, probably not worth attempting.

The next Sunday, my parents came to take me out for the afternoon but I said: 'I wish you hadn't come.' So they went away. My father thought it was because I was having such a good time. My mother cried all the way home. I had done the sums: sixteen weeks of holiday, thirty-six weeks of term; I didn't have a home any more; I didn't have a family; I was on my own, with very limited defences in a hostile world. (I have probably never fully trusted another human being since.)

I began to walk in my sleep and complained of being ill. Doctors frowned over my symptoms but no one knew what was wrong, and the decline was a little too gradual to seem important; schoolmasters were certain I was 'slacking' for which the best cure was cold showers and cross-country runs; but my immune system had misclassified some of my more useful organs as alien bodies and was slowly and methodically destroying them. It was another eight years before the doctors finally stumbled across what was causing it, half my life; recovery was just as slow, and never more than partial (psychotic episodes are a common side effect of one of the remedial drugs).

My formal education had been a waste of time and money, but it was a relief to be finally declared 'ill', to have a good excuse for my behaviour.

If it hadn't been for the illness I might have been all right; intelligence alone should have more than compensated for all the other limitations. As it was, I didn't stand much of a chance. I became increasingly withdrawn, silent, rarely laughing (not like I used to), ever more trapped inside my own head, and not greatly enjoying the company.

Chapter 30

1960, 1987

It would be misleading to dismiss the school as a bad place or even as a place that I hated. If life was simpler it would be a lot easier.

At the end of each term [or possibly only at the end of the Christmas or summer term; I no longer remember], the masters put on a variety concert in the Old Hall which always ended with the headmaster, whose nickname was Joc, singing The School Beside the Bardwell Road, a variation on a music hall song of his university days, the lyrics amended to include satirical references to the school year [or term], but the high point, the one that everyone remembers, was always a master whose nickname was Jacko playing the banjo and singing 'Ivan Skavinski Skavar'. Occasionally I hear it on the radio programme Desert Island Discs and know immediately where the guest had been to school. (Do guests on Desert Island Discs ever request Eric Coates's Lazy Lagoon, the programme's signature tune, as one of their favourite pieces of music? Or would it be forbidden because casual listeners might assume the programme had come to an end and switch off?)

At the end of my last term I stood on the balcony watching the concert beside a friend called Clive Charles, who a few days later would go out of my life for ever (the balcony from where sixty years earlier, a boy called Ned Morphew had fallen to his death; thirty years later I called my son Ned after him, for reasons I cannot begin to understand). Clive had tears running down his face: 'We will always remember this,' he said.

For good or bad, the school has been a rock (a place of temporary salvation and the cause of the original shipwreck), one of the few fixed points in my life; for many years, I knew it would always be there: I only had to go back (not that I often did) to find that nothing had changed, as though I had never been away.

You never stopped being a part of the school. Some twenty-five years after I left, the telephone rang on my office desk and a voice said: 'Hello Ben. Guv here,' my favourite member of staff, a junior teacher when I had been at the school, much later joint headmaster. I hadn't spoken to him in ten years, or more, but it seemed entirely normal to find him on the other end of the telephone. (Guv wanted permission to run extracts from my father's posthumously published autobiography in the school magazine. Yes, of course he could.)

Despite its many virtues, the school and all the others like it (similar but not so good) produced only two basic types. One was shy, diffident, damaged, unable to relate to other people or understand his own emotional responses. Many of the masters who taught there were like that – they were not bad people; far from it, some could be described as exceptionally good, when judged on their intentions, just unaware they were helping to perpetuate a system in which they themselves had also been the victims.

The other type were loud, brash, natural leaders (bullies), unable to relate to other people and uninterested in their own emotional responses (most of the other masters who taught there were like that). In years past people like that ran the 'empire', with predictable results. Now most of them are involved in making money (and wrecking the country's economy in the process).

A few years back, I went to a school reunion; unfortunately, almost all the other 'old boys' attending the event were of the second type, the ones I least wanted to meet again (although at the age of ten or twelve it was often difficult to tell which camp they would eventually fall into), all of them earning absurd amounts of money and never doubting they deserved it (and more), all with the word 'financial' in their job titles, all looking identical, holding identical opinions in loud voices, all wanting the same things. Once they were too scared to break ranks; now they could no longer imagine why anyone would ever want to. But when they told me their names I could still recognise the boys they used to be, when they were almost real people with separate distinct identities, damaged children crying with homesickness; they haven't really changed: they are still there hiding beneath thick shells; but people like that always believed in safety in numbers and always will.

Chapter 31

2011, 1997

We are living, for the present (living for nothing), in an old cathedral city on the border of England and Wales. I don't know why. We know no one and have no obvious connection with the place. Neither of us is working – in free fall, without visible or invisible means of support. Our flat is large and strange, very light and airy, probably cold in winter, on the top floor of an almost completely deserted mansion block, once a hospital. Among the former residents was the great self-taught ornithologist Dr Reg Moreau who died, possibly in my bedroom, in 1972; in his last letter he wrote about the house martins, hirondelles de fenêtre, that nested under the eaves by the window, and still do. His major work, the one he is remembered for, was a the definitive study of the African lives of migrating species, some of whom break their journey on my island. (House martins nested in the shed in my father's last garden, a very exposed site for a nest, only head high and vulnerable to anyone using the shed; they didn't mind him but after he died they never returned.)

Another resident, although only for six weeks in 1960 was Michael Foot in the aftermath of a near-fatal road crash. He spent his time in his hospital bed reading Montaigne. I don't know where his ward was.

The long vaulted corridors are reminiscent of The Shining or Bergman's The Silence, or possibly Last Year in Marienbad; in the first month, I saw three other people, one of whom might have been a cleaner. (The lights outside our door suddenly spring into life as I step out into the empty corridor, something of a shock until I get used to it.)

There are worse places to be. Our living room looks out over gardens, a large lime tree and the river, which is constantly changing while always remaining reassuringly the same. Heraclitus famously said that no man ever steps in the same river twice (the water is always changing, and you are no longer the person you were when you last saw it). The Japanese have a similar aphorism of a slightly later date, usually assumed to be a case of someone coming up with the same idea independently, but this is not necessarily so: I once came across a statue of Poseidon in a Kyoto temple and realised that the silk road would have carried two-way traffic (in intellectual as well as material property).

On rainy days, people holding umbrellas, or sometimes riding bicycles (but never doing both at the same time), cross the white wrought-iron pedestrian bridge, an elegant Victorian folly built to celebrate an earlier Jubilee but more reminiscent of a Hokusai print; sometimes it catches the morning sunlight when everything else is in shade. The view of the bridge in the morning light is, I would [probably grudgingly] concede, an ever-changing delight; much later, I wish I had taken more notice of it, that I hadn't turned my back on it, as I always do to all the things that fail to meet my initial approval, preferring to sulk rather than make the best of things, a bad trait I really should have grown out of. I should have photographed the bridge, river and trees, with a tripod always in the same position (the left-hand living room window looking upstream), recording how the light changes through the seasons, but I never thought I would be here so long. Maybe I should include the window frame in the picture and mount six frames on a single card spaced to match the panes of the window. [But I don't.]

Every day, the swans paddle slowly upstream then fly noisily back down; the seagulls float with the stream and fly back up. Only a person with nothing better to do would notice this. Dr Moreau would have noticed and known why (probably something to do with seagulls being scavengers relying on food thrown from the bridge whereas swans have some legitimate food source in the river best found by slowly paddling upstream). Of course, the seagulls may not have been here in Moreau's time, only migrating this far inland as the trawler industry declined.

The bridge crosses the river to a park, where the autumn colours are very Japanese; the cathedral is immediately to the right, the only building in sight, but almost entirely obscured by the trees, and only visible at all if you lean out the window (rarely a good idea). From the windows on the other side of the apartment you can see fields with cows; the closeness of the river and the danger of flooding has protected this small enclave from the mindless tide of excessive development that has engulfed the rest of the city and most other English towns. When signing the rental lease to the flat, I was seriously pissed off to find it was obligatory for me to insure its (non-existent) contents and that the minimum premium would be double the standard rate because of the proximity of the river: the flat is on the second floor and the river would have to rise by at least sixty feet to get anywhere near the carpet by when half of southern England would be underwater and the insurance company and its underwriters would already have filed for bankruptcy or fled the country. Seriously pissed off.

Ducks and seagulls perch on the window ledges.

I can walk to the city centre in five minutes. There are many ugly things in the city, even more than in most large towns and cities, but I have no contact with any of them, at least none of the modern ones, on my journey along the river bank and across Castle Green. In the early years of the Wars of the Roses a 'traitor' was executed there, perhaps where elderly men in white flannels play bowls, or maybe I walk over the actual spot (although I fail to notice a sudden drop in temperature that often clings to such places). According to a contemporary account, the traitor remained impassive while his penis and testicles were cut off and burnt before his eyes but when his belly was slit open and his intestines pulled out he gave a single howl of anguish 'to the great merriment of the crowd'. Sometimes I do not like the human race.

Beyond Castle Green my route leads through the cathedral grounds and down an ancient alleyway (signs in the pet shop window advertise 'Wild bird seed' and 'Frozen dog food'; what do you feed a frozen dog? Perhaps a dozen frogs?), emerging suddenly through an archway into the carless city centre (through caverns measureless to man down to a carless sea). Unfortunately once you get to the middle, there is not much to see or do, much like in the maze at Hampton Court. The shops are largely identical to those you would find in most other provincial cities, but possibly worse, most of them slowly going out of business. Even the charity shops are closing. Two bored Peruvian buskers launch into Il Condor Pasa for the twentieth time this morning, their enthusiasm diminishing with every note. The town is dying too.

The pedestrianised city centre was a concept much loved by town planners in the eighties and nineties but somehow it fails to deliver any valuable new space. It just seems like any other city street with a mysterious and very temporary absence of cars and inappropriate herringbone paving; if they had planted a few hundred trees instead of leaving the space blank it might have helped, but it is probably too late now.

At night everything changes, but I am rarely there to see it. The town centre fills with feral youth in all their improbable and – in the sombre season – inadequate finery, boys and girls shouting, fighting, shagging in doorways, vomiting and urinating in the streets, worshippers of the stranger god. Like the Molochs in The Time Machine, they only come out at night, vanishing before morning.

My daughter, visiting for the week, buys a copy of The Rings of Saturn at the bookshop. 'That's made my day; he's my favourite author after Borges,' says the woman at the till, but even I can see behind her smile that she has lost her way. Her twenties have drifted into her thirties, somehow bypassing all her long-hoped-for achievements or consolations, even the minor ones that few other people would have wanted, cared about or begrudged her. ('Go to the island,' I want to say, but don't.)

My daughter tells her she is writing a dissertation about both Sebald and Borges (on the artistic interpretation of time, or some such) and the woman says: 'I wish I could change places with you.' Perhaps everyone who lives in this town has lost their way: perhaps if they hadn't, they wouldn't be living here, a town of 'I'd rather be...' (This is not necessarily so, of course, none of it really. As I said before, the imaginary inner landscape bears so little relationship to objective reality that it is best treated as fiction.)

The city's intellectual and cultural life is entirely in the past. Alfred Watkins of The Long Straight Track used to live round the corner, a plaque on the river bank marks the spot where a long time ago a dog famously fell into the river, and the seventeenth-century mystic Thomas Traherne is buried in the cathedral, whose prize possession is a medieval circular map of the world that you wouldn't really want to rely on to get from A to B. Crete is easily identifiable from the outline of a labyrinth taking up most of the island but I look in vain for a small triangular dot just below it (although above and below – like north, south, east and west – have less precise meanings in maps like these). Not that I expected it to be there; by the fourteenth century my island had effectively disappeared from history and mythology. Saracen pirates made their home in Sarakiniko bay, and pirates don't make good neighbours. Perhaps a few people still lived in Kastri – the name would suggest a castle or some way of defending yourself against predatory intruders but if the castle was ever built nothing remains – but most of the islanders would have left for the relative safety of Crete.

The local museum above the library houses a very random assortment of objects, not least an alarming collection of Victorian proctology instruments side by side with the bones of a circus elephant – it was leading a parade just before the first world war and dropped dead in the High Street, probably of exhaustion; I feel a certain affinity with it. (And what will happen to the boy when the circus comes to town?)

One of the few things we bring from storage is a painting that the removal people neglected to wrap properly; it was leaning against a wall on a concrete floor, not a fit place for an oil painting, even a not very good one. I had never really looked at it before, or more likely had never hung it where it might be properly appreciated. But in the flat, the previous tenant had left some hooks in the walls and without giving the matter much thought I hung the picture at the end of a corridor at head height which was what it had always needed.

It is a landscape of the south of France – path, stone cottage, hillside, spring blossom, blue sea in the distance, reflections of boats, all the usual stuff; it is signed L Potronat and dated 1963, a present to my father from his insurance broker for reasons that are no longer possible to fathom: my father had many unusual interests but insurance was not one of them. Originally it came with a very 1960s frame, the kind you now only see on bad reproductions in charity shops; it used to hang in the living room of the cottage where my mother died, but it never looked right: people would glance at it and shake their heads; they thought it belonged on a chocolate box or a jigsaw. When I inherited the picture, Jenny had it re-framed, but it wasn't much better so we stuck it out of the way above a door where no one really noticed it. Perhaps all it needed to be in the right place, or to be looked at in the right frame of mind.

It is, when you eventually notice it, an accomplished, if modest, piece of painting. As you walk towards it along the corridor, it has a Narnia-like ability to draw you into its private world, a world that has stopped around 1880: modern art does not exist, not even Seurat or Cezanne. L Potronat had nothing very original to say about light, colour or composition but he knew better than most, through decades of practice, how many brush strokes it takes to portray a convincing cypress tree, or the way heat reflects off terracotta roof tiles. (But he probably painted the sky and the hills beyond the bay on automatic pilot.) Potronat produced virtually the same picture for last seventy years of his life; all the vicissitudes of the twentieth century were excluded from his field of vision and he reverted to the certainties of his childhood.

The cows have disappeared from the field on the other side of the flat; a surprisingly brief story in the local newspaper reports that a cow in that very same farm has died of anthrax, the country's first recorded case in twenty years. Then there is nothing; the story itself dies in suspicious circumstances. I look hopefully for echoes of Death in Venice but fail to find any: no sudden absence of foreign papers in the newsagents – they were never any there in the first place – no hearses in the night, no mysterious odour of carbolic emanating from the Peruvian buskers. But the cows haven't returned.

As I step out into the corridor, the lights no longer spring into action with quite the same sense of urgency; they are like soldiers reluctantly saluting an officer who has lost authority, my temporary kingship nearing the end of its tenure; they are playing the game of seeing how far they can go along the line of insubordination without being put on a charge.

Perhaps I have unwittingly encroached on a taboo I never realised existed; somehow a bond with the outside world has been broken and not easily mended. I long ago gave up asking other people whatever it was that they thought I had done that was wrong – it only ever makes things worse; one of the many things I am expected to know without asking, but rarely do. Almost never do. A part of me doesn't understand, has never understood. I always fail to see the early signs of other people's disappointment, embarrassment or irritation. I never expect the storm before it breaks.

I sometimes dream that I am 'blind', that everything I assume to be part of the outside world is just a product of my imagination; I only discover this by accident when I start bumping into 'invisible' walls and pieces of furniture.

Sometimes you think you are travelling on the train and then suddenly without knowing why you find yourself standing on the wrong platform at the wrong stop watching the train go past, and there is nothing you can do about it.

Chapter 32

2010

'Yes, it often happens like that,' says Thomasina, the neurologist at St Thomas' Hospital. 'You just have to live with it; get into a routine where you can do an hour or two's writing a day.' She gives me some pills to help me stay awake.

I tell the endocrinologist about when I was sixteen and dying in the Radcliffe Infirmary in Oxford. My condition conformed to none of the usual textbook illnesses, my symptoms hopelessly confused by nearly a decade of incorrect treatment, so the avuncular, Dickensian physician in charge my case, a Mr Cook (for some no doubt special reason Mr not Dr), decided to give me the minimum of medication in the hope that the picture would eventually become clearer and some proper symptoms might emerge. It was a close-run thing: when eventually he was confident enough to put a name to my condition I was incapable of sitting up in bed without passing out from exhaustion, probably about four weeks from death. There is something I remember, something forgotten for many years, and since it resurfaced a cause of minor puzzlement, something that has never been properly explained: one afternoon when I was just beginning to get better, I woke to hear Mr Cook and some visiting physicians standing at the foot of my bed discussing my case (the first they had ever had at the hospital, and a source of some academic interest); Mr Cook said that what had finally alerted him was the discovery that my heart was half the normal size.

I tell the story to the endocrinologist but she shakes her head and smiles. 'It doesn't affect the size of your heart,' she says. Perhaps it wasn't a real memory, just something I dreamed.

The amiable, balding, curly-haired psychiatrist checking for brain damage becomes increasingly puzzled as I solve all his problems with ease. 'No one's got that one right in twenty years,' he mutters, the hairs on the side of his head curling like question marks.

Fortunately all the non-verbal problems are two-dimensional. I have more trouble with three-dimensional ones, my mind confusing the issue by unintentionally inventing extra spacial dimensions, like a pyramid growing a new pyramid on each of its facets, the pattern constantly threatening to repeat itself infinitely. The problem of how to deal with this – whether to simplify or let it reach an inevitable conclusion – is not easily resolved. Faced with the hydra which grew two new heads whenever one was cut off, Hercules and Iolos chose to cauterise the stump with a burning torch to prevent regrowth; they could equally have carried on chopping until the hydra became a perfect sphere of mouths without the space to open, like an orange pomander covered in cloves.

Once I tried to write a novel that would have the complexity and layers of meaning of other novels I admired; I didn't realise that complexity was inevitable, that I could only arrive at where I wanted to be by simplifying as much as I could, and that by aiming for density my novel would rapidly become unreadable.

But there are anomalies. The psychiatrist reads out a word from a list and I have to come up with another word that has no connection with it; this is impossible until I hit on the stratagem of thinking up the answer before hearing the cue word, which defeats the object of the exercise, and ever then it doesn't always work: everything connects whether I want it to or not – I see endless similarities between unlikely things but I am no good at identifying differences; I am incapable of classifying anything because I have no basis for classification. One thing leads inevitably to another and eventually back to where it started. Filling in forms has become almost impossible: every question has a dozen different but (to me) equally plausible answers, although probably none that would have occurred to the people compiling the form.

I am as guilty of self-deception as anyone, probably more so (inconvenient facts ignored and quickly forgotten; self-interest masquerading as duty; other things), but I am for some reason incapable of saying or thinking anything that I consciously know to be false, no matter how sensible – or even polite – it would be to do so, a bit like the Memory Man in the film of The Thirty-Nine Steps.

Jorge Luis Borges much preferred the film of The Thirty-Nine Steps to the book even though the latter uses a literary conceit that ought to have appealed to him: that if you pretend with sufficient confidence you can persuade other people to accept almost anything. In the book, the villain turns up at the War Office claiming to be a senior admiral, to whom he bears little physical resemblance; he is admitted, without questions asked, into a top-secret security meeting in the company of the other defence chiefs all of whom know the admiral well but somehow fail to notice anything unusual, and at the end of the meeting he leaves the building with Britain's defence secrets in his briefcase. It is nonsense by any standards, and could never have worked on film any more than in real life, but the author, John Buchan, just about manages to get away with it in the book simply by pretending that it is an entirely reasonable possibility and saying so with sufficient confidence that the reader is carried along.

I might have been one of the few people to be taken in by the villain as I am having trouble with my visual memory; I find it increasingly difficult to recognise people, even people I know well if I meet them in unexpected places. I have several times accosted James Le Fanu, the doctor and very good writer, under the mistaken impression that he was James Meek, the former Guardian journalist and also very good writer, or quite possibly it was the other way round; either way, they were baffled by the encounter and the coincidence of the same first names meant they didn't automatically assume it to be a case of mistaken identity. I don't know if they have any obvious physical resemblance; presumably there must be something.

I am also, and apparently always was, dyslexic. I had often wondered why I was such a hopeless proofreader, a terminal disadvantage for anyone trying to earn a living as an editor: at the best of times, my brain has been subconsciously guessing one word in four and when tired, as I usually am when working, it gets much worse; I have read books all my life, but never with the fluency other people appear to manage, and the books as I understand and later remember them may be very different from how they are understood by other people or intended by the author.

At school I was very good at reading the lesson in chapel but only after rehearsing the text repeatedly in my head. Once the headmaster unexpectedly singled me out to recite Kubla Khan for the benefit of some important visitor – 'I think this is one for you, Mallalieu,' he said – and I stumbled in a deeply embarrassing fashion; my over-long hesitation after '… the earth in fast thick pants' was a cause of particular merriment among my peers; the headmaster assumed I had been doing it on purpose.

I am also dyspraxic and to some unspecified extent autistic. Not to mention attention deficit… something or other. The mind heads off at tangents; the centre cannot hold, sparking away like a catherine wheel. The compulsion to wander.

None of these terms were much in use during my formative years, never by people in authority over me; that all kicked in too late to be of any use. I had often suspected that I was, in some not easily defined way, 'different' or 'odd' but had always assumed that that was how most people felt: I occasionally in later years read accounts of Asperger's syndrome but without any sense of recognition, no sense of 'belonging' to whatever it was they were writing about, no sense of having been there before, no sudden realisation of the 'hey, that's me they're writing about' variety.

I become increasingly aware that I have never been very good at distinguishing right from wrong, relying too much on other people's opinions, too easily assuming they must be right and I wrong, trying too hard to adhere to a set of moral values I cannot fully understand, and ending up pleasing no one. I have a regrettable habit of saying 'yes' in response to anything anyone says, meaning 'I hear what you're saying' rather than, as they would reasonably assume, 'I agree with you'.

And I have never been any good at telling left from right, quite hopeless when trying to give Jenny directions in the car. I am confused by the knowledge that what is 'right' to me is 'left' to someone coming in the opposite direction, who probably has right of way. Somewhere in my brain, the mirror image of an object exists with equal validity. I long ago gave up trying to remember whether screws, nuts and bolts need to be turned clockwise or anticlockwise.

As I am leaving, the psychiatrist taps my skull and says: 'Look after that brain of yours. It's special.'

Unfortunately it really doesn't work as well as it should, certainly not as well as it used to: the reasoning process has become opaque (cataracts of the mind). I open the door of the dumb waiter and on a good day I find an idea inside, fully finished, sitting on a plate to be used or rejected, a message from the deeper recesses of my brain over which I have less and less control, no fine tuning permitted or possible. Ideas appear (or don't) with the finality of the letters from the 'masters' that the splendid old occultist Madame Blavatsky claimed had materialised in her cupboard.

More and more often my cupboard is bare, and I know nothing.

Like Niccolo Machiavelli, I hold lengthy conversations in my head with people who aren't there; but if they were there my mind would empty, shut up shop, and I would have nothing to say.

Sometimes I think the world has been changed while I slept, replaced by one that is in every superficial way identical but fundamentally alien (although no one else appears to have noticed).

The newspapers mostly contain accounts of nasty events over which I have no control, or articles about people and things about which I know little and care nothing. This is not my world. North, south, east and west mean nothing to me now.

Chapter 33

2011

A deceptive sea mist obscures the horizon, forming an invisible join between the clear blue sky and the clear blue sea. Behind the ferryboat, Crete has already disappeared; ahead, the island is nowhere to be seen; half a mile away a Breughel-like fishing boat, a ship of fools, floats in the sky, half a dozen seagulls circling around, above and, so it almost looks, below.

The day before I left England, the island's new 'Express' ferry was suddenly cancelled 'until further notice'; the mail boat has unexpectedly left on time, too soon for me to catch it; but strangely, and not mentioned in any of the schedules, a little ship with the – for Greece – improbable name of Neptune is running each Saturday between Sougia and the island. Old and slow, it might easily have been pensioned off after many years taking day trippers round the bay in some faded English South Coast resort; possibly a 'little ship' that lost its way on the passage to Dunkirk in 1940. Somehow it has managed to pass under the radar of the scrutineers. [Apparently, it used to be the island's main ferry until it was decommissioned in the 1980s and left to rot in Souda bay then hurriedly done up and put back in service in the wake of last year's latest ferry fiasco – the shipping company bought a new ferry from Japan, no doubt at great expense, sent out a crew to collect it only to find that no one had checked whether the draught was shallow enough to enter the harbour, and it wasn't.]

'Please let the bus be there,' I say to myself as the Neptune rounds the mole, but it isn't, as I always knew it wouldn't be. The bus driver is there, of course, and he greets me like an old friend.

'Bus kaput,' he says. He speaks little English; perhaps 'problemo' and 'kaput' are his only two foreign words, probably all he needs – enough for anyone to get by with in most circumstances. Since last year, he has dyed his hair an unconvincing shade of blond.

Anastasia from the taverna waves as I begin the weary trudge, pack on back, up the hill.

For the usual complex family reasons, Sophia's Taverna is no longer Sophia's. Nor is it a taverna. The covered terrace has been demolished, but a new one, virtually identical but bigger, is being built further up the hill. 'When will it open?' I ask Sophia's brother Pavlos. 'Next week, perhaps,' he says. 'Next week' is a flexible term in Greece, easily confused with 'next month' and 'never'.

The Portakabin has been decked out in mock-Tyrolean/Hawaiian style with a cladding of varnished split-pine logs and wood-effect paint on the flat metal surfaces; the corrugated plastic awning has been underslung with bamboo. It is now a cafe run by a large friendly Cretan called Costas, and surprisingly busy, but at first glance I see no one I know. A Greek hippie with blond dreadlocks is waiting at tables, and from a distance he looks like my old friend Panos – he has the same easy-going elegance seldom far from self-parody, moving with cat-like tread, leaping recumbent dogs, tray of food in one hand, glass of rum in the other, large roll-up in mouth – but he isn't.

The Portakabin is not the kind of place you would travel for three days just to visit, but the beer is cold, the prices no worse than last year, the view looks out over the tops of the junipers and across the sea to the mountains of Crete, and the company is congenial. There are many worse places to be.

Chapter 34

2011

From my eyrie under the tree, my dusty bower, I can see the whole length of the beach, two hundred yards to the right, four hundred to the left.

At 3am it is covered with a thick layer of mist; I lean out of my hammock to see an eiderdown of cloud ten feet below.

5am: The mist has gone. The sky is already blue, a sickle moon due east and immediately below it a single bright star or planet (Venus?). Then exactly between the two I can just make out another much smaller planet; nothing else in the entire sky. Years ago, an old friend from Tehran called Martin Shanahan insisted we should all meet up the following year on a hillside in Peru because on a particular morning an unusual number of planets would be perfectly aligned for the first time in an enormous number of years. I never realised what he meant, that it might be something you could actually see. I never went; I don't suppose he did either.

6.30am: Early morning resembles an Edvard Munch twilight; the dot of the sun rising above an invisible Crete to form a lower-case 'i', its long reflection serifed on the horizon.

7am: I brush my teeth in the sea and walk along the deserted beach. Crete is still out of sight, one seagull, no ships, the sea flat and circular: the world is a flat disc of no more than fifty miles diameter, the island a little off centre to the north. I look for pieces of shell resembling sharks teeth, only ever found in one short section of the beach, and shards of glass rounded at the edges and frosted like Lalique.

Horizons shrink: first the world, then the island, then the beach, then the hammock, then the book.

7.45am: A slightly intimidating Maria Callas-like Greek woman walks along the beach from the left, a thin blue shawl over her shoulders and thick black hair curling halfway down her back. She is followed by what looks like a small group of blackbirds swooping close to the sand in an intricate, constantly changing pattern. It takes a while to realise that it is a single black-and-white dog bounding extravagantly, not like a real dog, more like a dog in a cartoon film.

Actually she is not intimidating at all; that is just a superficial impression from fifty yards away. Close to, despite a persistent resemblance to Medea in the Pasolini film, she is a dear person and we talk most mornings. She often describes at length in very broken English the plots of British films I have never heard of; she is a particular fan of the works of Guy Ritchie – very unlike Medea. She has a Mayan calendar tattooed on her upper arm and something in Elvish on her bottom.

I remember the friendly old man I often saw in the streets around my school in north Oxford. He lived what seemed at the time a very ordinary life in an ordinary Victorian house and in his spare time wrote intellectually obscure fantasies on the borderline of what was considered commercially viable; his plans to write a history of the Elvish tongue were not encouraged by his publishers so he wrote The Lord of the Rings instead. There were no naked women in his books, and conspicuously few wearing clothes. Did he ever imagine the parts his words would reach? What would he have made of it?

8.15am: O'Connor strides purposefully along the beach like a clockwork beetle. ('Hello O'Connor,' I say. 'Who?' he replies, and I have to apologise: 'Sorry, that's the name I've given you in this book.')

8.20am: Two Austrian women, one blonde in an orange sarong, the other dark in blue, walk from the east to swim directly below me, fifty yards away. Some people are very good at swimming, but it is impossible to predict whom (they both are). Some people have an elegance of movement in water that they never possess on land. I flap about in the sea like a fish out of water; I swim well underwater, surprisingly well, but I never mastered the business of swimming along the surface, when to breathe in and out and suchlike. Perhaps I was too ill at the age when all my friends were learning to do it properly.

8.30am: A jogger in black shorts begins the first of his morning sixty lengths of the beach. He has an easy, upright, very correct running style, head still, like an athlete in a 1950s East European propaganda film.

I have found that another creature is exploring the beach at night leaving tracks like a miniature bicycle tyre; as soon as I first notice them I begin to see them everywhere, even in the sand under my hammock; I can identify the imprint of tiny feet and what appears to be a tail: some kind of lizard perhaps. Scorpions would be a less welcome possibility, but very unlikely. There are plenty of beetles but when I watch one it leaves no trace.

And something else is making perfect cone-shaped depressions in the sand under the tree, about three inches across and one deep, sometimes smaller. (On the small beach on the way to Lavrakas, the one where I met Anna standing alone and Aphrodite-like in the water, I found a line of footprints like no other, each a pair of adjoining equilateral triangles, like a double-headed axe.)

I open my rucksack and the largest spider I have ever seen in Europe runs out, most unsettling even though I know it to be harmless (probably); fortunately, it is as keen as I am put some distance between us. Perhaps it has a family to go to.

9am: A crocodile of four small children, too alike in height and age to be all siblings, too similar not to be cousins, march down to the sea – the first in red, the second striped in blue and white, the third in orange, the fourth naked – suddenly breaking ranks, turning and running back when called from their unseen encampment in the trees; an old-fashioned scene stirring memories of family holidays long ago, not so much my own although I have a brief flashback of Alan Gibson's younger son sitting in the sea at Hope Cove wearing a bright yellow sou'wester. Perhaps it is an EH Shepherd illustration to an AA Milne poem [more likely the Helen Oxenbury illustrations to We're Going on a Bear Hunt].

10am: The sea is wild today. In the lee of a reef at the start of the beach, the sea has scooped out a deep pool in the sand only a few yards from the shore (elsewhere the beach shelves gently, often tediously). I sit in the pool while the waves crash on the rocks spraying plumes of foam six foot into the air. The water is turquoise, so full of bubbles that you suspect a cupped handful might fizz away almost to nothing.

I am joined by Dr Iorgos who usually spends his summers studying the island's insects and other creatures, peering into rock pools on under stones wearing an ancient canvas hat and a black cotton sarong, almost an academic gown, thrown over his shoulders (sometimes when the wind blows the rim of his hat up he looks like a Mexican desperado). He holds unusual opinions which he expresses diffidently. He says the the conventional dating of the island's trees is wrong: the oldest are not five hundred but fifteen hundred years old and many would be as old as five thousand if the Romans hadn't cut them down for temple roofs and the Venetians hadn't used the rest as piles for their city.

The rocks around this part of the coast are mostly the same jagged sandstone but at the start of the beach is a brief stretch of about thirty yards where their surface is smooth and the pattern of gullies running between them more ornate. Iorgos says they must have been carved by hand and there is no other obvious explanation. If so, it must have been done in Classical or Minoan times before earthquakes lowered this end of the island (the carvings stretch thirty yards into and under the sea). Why anyone would have chosen to do this is not clear (possibly for launching boats, but probably not). Erik von Daniken, had he seen them, might have concluded that they were an ancient computer but he would have been wrong – I think we can say that with reasonable confidence, although I have always had a fondness for Erik von Daniken, not because of his theories, of course, which were tosh, but because he was a fellow outsider. Academics hated him because without any formal training to give him respectability, he had encroached on their territory and made a large amount of money (which they would much rather had gone to them); the Swiss government hated him because he became famous internationally for holding ideas that were considered unsound and might adversely affect the nation's reputation for probity and sober judgement (making it less attractive to the money launderers and other financial criminals they depend on) – they even hounded him for minor tax offences that more respectable members of Swiss society would not have hesitated to commit.

10.30am: On my way home I call on Athena and Marina whom I met yesterday where they were trying and failing to put up their tent – small spikes attached to the groundsheet fitted snugly into sockets at the end of the tent poles, an unusual arrangement that had not occurred to them. The elder, Athena, is an actress with curly very Greek hair; Marina is half-American, does something designerish and has straight hair (with a hair slide of the kind worn by American teenagers in the 1950s); otherwise they look very similar, with identical tattoos, although in different places. Athena is reading aloud from Thus Spake Zarathustra in Greek but she stops when I arrive so we can chat, which is a pity as I would like to hear Nietzsche in Greek, even though I don't know what it means. (I don't know what it means in English; it just sounds good.) As I leave Marina says with old New World courtesy: 'Thank you for visiting.' ('… and please won't you call back again'.)

11am: Two people walk along the beach exactly in step. As they pass, their bodies align with my line of sight and their tread goes out of phase; just for a moment they look like one person with a multiplicity of wobbly legs joined at the knee. A long-haired dachshund emerges from the water resembling a sodden giant millipede.

The sea is a series of uneven stripes of light and dark, like the rings of Saturn: a thin dark line on the horizon, then a broad light strip, then thin medium, broad light, broad medium. In five minutes the pattern will be different, although the sickle blade of bright water closer to the island will still be there, a current perhaps.

Noon: A blind minotaur-like rembetika player, with bullish head and grizzled beard, makes his way slowly but confidently alone to the water's edge. Is he unaware of the beautiful women he passes by or does he see them all, and more, in his mind's eye? (I was once invited to a reception at 10 Downing Street – only once, certainly never again – and half way through the evening I looked up and was for a moment disconcerted to find the then Home Secretary David Blunkett staring at me from the other side of the room.)

I can now see Crete again through the haze.

Most lunchtimes and evenings I walk to Costas's Portakabin/cafe, but rarely, if ever, by the same route twice. I know the general direction and recognise familiar landmarks, but they seldom recur in the same order twice – the larger tree with the tall upright bole; the one with the long horizontal branch from which half a dozen new trees are beginning to sprout resembling a market stall of forgotten pot plants; a root above ground spanning a narrow pathway where one day soon I will trip over in the dark; the broken camp where my friends Louis and Kristina, Panos, Nadia and the others lived four years ago. Mostly the landscape repeats itself: hedgehogs of thyme, lentisk and rock rose, larger mounds of pine and juniper, then mountain and sea, plenty of honeycomb rock and sand, more than enough.

One afternoon I follow a pair of footprints thinking the owner must have known the best route only to realise they are my own, still there from this morning, or yesterday.

The rocks resemble a Max Ernst landscape of the Europe After the Rains era, mud whipped up by a storm then baked hard and sharp by some sudden nuclear catastrophe. Subsequent centuries of rain have failed to soften the edges. Perhaps this area was once forest destroyed by fire and the topsoil washed away, or is the concept of eroded landscapes just a myth as most modern authorities claim? The sand on the beach and in the dunes doesn't get washed away, but it has, of course, very different properties: it doesn't form a hard crust when dry and then when wet dissolve into a semi-liquid suspension, but why roots should hold the soil together is not clear. Perhaps the canopy protects the surface from the full blast of the rainfall.

(Eventually, I opt in daylight to take the northern route along the rocks close to the sea, the longer way round but with less chance of getting lost and the breeze is better; at night I go south over the dunes – less chance of damage if I fall over.)

Conversation with a Greek hippie:

Me: 'Kalimera.'

Hippie: 'Hey man.'

2pm: I return from the taverna to find that the goats have helped themselves to my emergency food – peanuts, dried apricots, biscuits – even eating most of the wrapping paper. All they have left is an unopened bag of dried figs and half a bar of Kendal's Mint Cake covered in sand (caked in sand?). Do goats not like figs? I don't any more and can't think why I brought them with me: once hitching home broke from Istanbul I had to survive for almost the whole journey (including two and a half bad days in Yugoslavia without a single lift) on dried figs and hazelnuts and I have never enjoyed eating them since; I don't like hazelnuts either.

I may have solved the mystery of the tracks on the beach. Beside my hammock a beetle is dragging away the last of my peanuts, the extra weight causing its legs to sink into the sand, the nut making the impression of a tail. (Apart from the peanut, I have never seen a beetle carrying anything or doing anything of a practical or self-improving nature.)

These beetles are, I am told, *Dendarus maximus* and are apparently unique to the island, although other than that I have so far failed to discover anything interesting about them. I sometimes tell people that the island is home to an unusual species of flying snail but they don't believe me, probably with good reason, although many Greek islands have a history of unusual animals. On Tilos, a shell from a wartime British destroyer opened the entrance of a cave that had been closed for 6,000 years. There in 1971, an archaeologist found the fossilised bones of dwarf elephants, the size of Shetland ponies, the first ever found in Europe, I was told [a bit of an exaggeration]. They had sheltered there from a volcano erupting in Nissiros or Santorini, the same that wrecked the Minoan civilisation on Crete, and were trapped by the lava. The current theory is that the elephants arrived on Tilos having swum all the way from Africa, which at first seems hardly credible, although animals often do unlikely things (giraffes are the only mammals that cannot swim long distances – something to do with their necks – or so it is said).

There is also the strange case of the Tilos tiger, as Dr Watson might have said; a pregnant female, survivor of a shipwrecked Victorian circus, was washed up on the uninhabited western shore and her descendants, interbreeding and growing increasingly smaller, have been there ever since, preying on a the local goats; unfortunately this story is untrue, originating no more than ten years ago in at Sofia's Restaurant in the port, an invention of Sofia's son Vasilis.

Actually, I now find that almost all the beetles are leaving trails; the one I watched this morning must have been unusually light-footed or the sand it was walking on untypically hard. But nothing explains the cone-shaped indentations under the tree.

A large moth – somewhere between a moth and a beetle, sand coloured – lands heavily on my arm. Instinctively I flick it away then feel guilty so I pick it up and put it on a rock in the shade, from where it looks at me with an aggrieved expression.

3pm: A woman with long red-brown hair and flowing black dress, a Pre-Raphaelite in mourning, sits motionless staring out to sea. Sometimes she walks to the water's edge, slowly undresses, sometimes stopping for many minutes halfway, lost in thought, then eventually swimming off in the vague direction of Crete. She will do the same tomorrow at much the same time.

There is something sloth-like about her, perhaps just the colour of her hair and the slowness of her movements but maybe something else. I realise I know nothing about the mating habits of the sloth. The Victorian naturalist Charles Waterton says they have only one 'inferior opening' like a bird, but he may be wrong. The off-white magician and generally bad person to know, Aleister Crowley once wrote that the idea of women priests was absurd because they had the incorrect number of bodily openings for conducting the mass. What did he mean, and is this the real cause of the Catholic church's objection?

I remember reading that sloths are surprisingly elegant swimmers; did Waterton know that?

4pm: Dr Iorgos tells me that the cone-shaped indentations are ant traps, literally pitfalls, dug by the ant-lion (myrmeleon, sometimes known as ant-griffin, a close relative of the equally mythical sounding owlfly); its larval form has the distinction of being the only insect without an anus. In America it known as doodlebug because of the patterns it draws in the sand. I don't know if I believe him.

5pm: The French couple from the next tree along stop as they walk past. 'Someone has been stealing little bits of food,' the man says in faltering English. 'We all need to be more careful.' So it wasn't the goats after all.

Does it matter? There is something a little endearing about a thief who only steals small amounts of food and is careful not to leave you entirely without, much like a house sprite. On both occasions when I was burgled in London I disliked most that my personal space had been encroached upon. Here, I have no private space and feel all the better for it. (The thief left it behind – the moon in the branches.)

Did St John the Divine steal little bits of food when he was a hermit on Patmos? Did any of Christ's locusts and wild honey come from the bags of other campers in the wilderness? Or the 'cake baken on the coals and a cruse of water' the angel brought to the distressed Elijah as he slept under his juniper tree. Did the ravens show him their receipts from Sainsbury's?

7.30pm: A solitary gull flies from west to east. I only ever see three gulls on this part of the island, this one and a breeding pair in Sarakiniko. I can see dozens from my window in the flat in the English city, a hundred miles inland (a long way east of Camberwell, spiritually if not geographically). I wonder what their relationship is. My half-empty plastic water bottle clicks (a very beetle-like sound) indicating an otherwise unnoticeable drop in temperature.

At dusk the air is suddenly full of large buzzing insects the size of bumble bees; they sound like bumble bees but fly too fast for proper identification, moving in mad patterns with no obvious sense to them, never quite landing, guarding their territory from rivals, buzzing you if you get too close. What are they after? Perhaps the same as the rest of us. Whatever that is.

9pm (when shadows pass gigantic on the sand): The Cretan hills first turn violet then slowly a very pale slate blue, dark at the edges like a solarised photograph. The sun contorts in odd shapes before it disappears, a bit like a baby's head at birth (as seen from the other direction). A white line marks where the waves break on the beach, then the sea darkens as it deepens. Three UFO-like clouds hover in the dip between the White mountains.

9.30pm: A man and canoe head off west towards Lavrakas, paddle silhouetted against the red sky. The surface of the water is beaten bronze.

The beach is silent apart from the waves; no people, and strangely no cicadas. There are plenty in Sarakiniko among the pines but few this year in the junipers. Years ago, I slept in an olive grove with cicadas invisible, but far from inaudible, on every branch. At first it was just white noise, then two began chirruping in unison, then three, then four, then five. For a brief moment around 3am all the cicadas in the grove were exactly in phase, then one broke rank, then two, then three, then four...

10pm: Someone is playing a guitar at the eastern end of the beach; I can also hear a flute and, elsewhere in the trees behind, a tabla caught only in snatches, the three instruments each probably inaudible to the others, drifting and intertwining, surprisingly harmonic when heard together, rising above the sound of the waves then sinking below, like dolphins.

Midnight: The sea is all a glimmer. In my room a forest grows and the walls become the world all around. No enemy but winter and rough weather. Where the Wild Things Are. Where I am.

Chapter 35

2011

One day I set off on a walk, a modest exercise: up the road towards Kastri before turning off to where Pieter last year pitched the Kalletechneion – it might still be there although he had been planning to move it to Ambelos on the far side of the island – then the path from the two shrines along the broken stream and through or over the Minoan town to Lavrakas, a two-hour round trip at most; and if it doesn't run to schedule I can rest through the midday heat on the beach in the shade.

But I should have known it is never going to work. It would have done once. But not now. By the time I reach the shrine of St Paul I am struggling, even worse than last year. Half way along the cart track to St Panteleimon I have had enough; I see an empty space where the Kalletechneion might have been but am too tired to investigate. Looking for and failing to find the fossil path from Agios Nikolaos I know I am lost. Uphill is desperately hard work; downhill is never as easy as you promised yourself it was going to be.

I know if I head downhill I will inevitably reach the sea. Unfortunately, the direct route is blocked by a gorge with a very sheer sixty-foot drop; once I would have tried to climb it (foolishly), but now it is no longer even worth thinking about. No option but to head back to higher ground until I can find an easier place to climb down, but, even then I have to climb back up the other side as there is no obvious way of descending right to the river bed – in the worst of the winter storms it would be just upstream from a high waterfall. Very soon I am confronted by another ravine, but this time the sides are gentler and I am able to reach the bed, although progress continues to be slow, mostly scrambling over boulders and landing ankle deep in mud. The river has been reduced to a series of stagnant terrapin pools, but not water anyone would want to drink. Some water is not worth getting thirsty for. Where do terrapins go in high summer when the pools dry up completely? Is there a summer equivalent of the word 'hibernate'? Perhaps they go to sea.

The time scale has gone seriously wrong. It is now the full heat of the day on the hottest day of the year so far by far. I measure out my steps, counting every one, to the next resting place then ration out my few remaining mouthfuls of water. I see a chapel but don't make the detour to find out which one it is. I know the old Minoan path is somewhere nearby but I fail to find any of the expected landmarks, neither the fossil track nor the site of the Minoan town; the magic passes me by. Another time, perhaps. I concentrate on watching my feet, careful where they tread.

Somewhere, I stumble into a whole grove of pink oleander stretching far above my head: it is not a plant I would want to cultivate – too much an automatic choice for lazy Mediterranean gardeners and town planners (you see them outside every airport and petrol station to no good effect) – but magnificent when they are where they belong. (Definitely not good on barbecues.)

Eventually out in the light in Lavrakas I no longer want to look for where Pieter had his camp last year, nor do I go to Solon's miraculous home beyond the headland; instead I lie face down in the water and wish it was colder. And from there to the well.

'No! No!' says a thin elegant Frenchman. 'You are doing it all wrong!'

I apologise very formally and the Frenchman shows me the correct way to lift the bucket, fill my bottle, pour the rest away, return the bucket while keeping the correct alignment of the lower sling swivel and retying the rope without contaminating the source water (I won't remember any of this next time or the time after).

When really thirsty, nothing tastes better than water. It doesn't even have to be cold.

I ask about Pieter and I am no longer a stranger: knowing Pieter grants me temporary membership of the club. The Frenchman has not seen him recently but he calls over an unkemptly bearded hippie with a shortage of teeth who says Pieter has been working on a house in Ambelos near the temple of Apollo. This is not a classical ruin but one of the Russians' more recent projects and a cause of a disproportionate amount of outrage from the Orthodox church; it has even made the national press in Athens, who ought to have had more important things to worry about. [Pieter says they should have built a temple of Dionysos: 'All you need is a tree and a bottle of wine.']

After another swim I fall into conversation on the beach with a Spanish woman who has spent all winter in the woods. I sit on my T shirt; she lies on the sand, the large gold crystals clinging to her wet body. I am conscious of being outside everything in a certain, awkward way while she participates with everything, 'allied to the forces of nature instead of against them'.

She has a powerful, possibly intimidating life force. Yesterday she went to Potomas to cut reeds for the roof of the shack she is building then walked back with a heavy load all in an hour and a half. What is it like here in winter? 'It is very special,' she says, which doesn't leave me much the wiser.

Rounding the headland on the way back to Agios Ioannis, I meet a man with curly sun-bleached blond hair.

'Kalimera,' I say.

'Wotcher mate,' he replies in a faux-working-class English accent, a bit of a shock as he is only the fourth British person I have met on the island although, when I think about it, he looks very much how I have always pictured the Englishman abroad, those of the Ben Gunn variety: he wears short saffron-coloured cotton shorts, a large gold earring and a string of broken shells like sharks teeth round his neck.

'Do you miss England?' he asks.

'No.'

'Nor me! I did the same job for twenty years and I was sick of it; one day I thought there had to be more to life than that, and there was. This place is perfect.'

He is an archetypal remittance man – now very much a vanished species although once common, at least in the stories of Somerset Maugham, Robert Louis Stevenson and Joseph Conrad. They were the undesirable younger sons of 'good' families who blotted their copybooks once too often and were packed off to the colonies with a small allowance – a remittance – on condition they never came back. Traditionally they lived in huts on beaches across the Pacific, drinking far too much of the local alcohol, marrying or not marrying local women and either way outraging the sensibilities of the local British community. In a typical Maugham story, a remittance man falls in love with a woman missionary, and sometimes one reforms the other and sometimes it is the other way round. (I may be imagining this, although I think there was a pre-war film with Charles Laughton along those lines.)

He could be one of the most contented people I have ever met.

Chapter 36

2011

Two days later, I try to hitch a lift to Ambelos but as bad luck would have it no cars are moving on this half of the island. I walk up through Kastri as far as the new lighthouse, and a deeply strange building it is, as odd as anything the Russians have built, although why this is so is not immediately obvious. When you first see it from a distance through the pine trees it looks brand new. Close to, it is already beginning to fray at the edges as though it has been suddenly deserted. New buildings are rarely abandoned except for sinister reasons – a staple of science fiction stories, the secret laboratory on a remote island where an unexpected but in retrospect horribly predictable disaster wipes out everyone except the unwitting protagonist (and possibly the odd genetically modified monster or two).

The truth is almost as strange. The original lighthouse was built by the Venetians and apparently the most powerful in Greece, putting the island's name quite literally back on the map after the dark ages, a source of local pride until the Germans destroyed it in the war. (That is the official story but I suspect it was the RAF.) When the EU started pumping money into absurd projects someone had the bright idea of rebuilding the lighthouse, no expense spared. But the light has never been switched on – apparently it would only confuse the sea traffic. A truly pointless exercise, a monument to the mad days at the turn of the twenty-first century, opened 2002, closed 1941 ('and in 1941...'). The light that failed at the end of the world.

I am about to climb over the wall to get a closer look when a slightly distracted woman holding a small child turns up out of nowhere to unlock the door. She says it is now a museum, with an exhibition of Greek lighthouses, and she runs what might possibly be called the café (a glass-fronted fridge with a few bottles of beer and tins of soft drinks, but the electricity is almost certainly not working). I ask about Pieter but she has never heard of him – if he is really living up here he would be her nearest neighbour – so I give up and walk back to Kastri.

The island's capital comprises some twenty houses, one smartish new hotel – the Princess – and a small taverna, very unsmart but the kind of place you go to Greece hoping to find. The walls are unfinished stone with no evidence of mortar; you wouldn't realise it was a taverna except for the sign on the door saying 'open'. Beyond it is a courtyard with a roof of reeds supported by bamboo poles; chicken-wire walls hang with vines, bougainvillea and a very exotic honeysuckle. Beyond is a proper garden, like a traditional English cottage garden with every inch planted with what looks like a random assortment of vegetables and ornamental plants. One shrub has long fluted leaves and yellow trumpet flowers. [What is it?] Distant views of the sea. Geraniums in old tins. Ancient wooden chairs freshly painted in matt colours: yellow, pale blue, maroon, purple, orange, light green, dark green, the colours of powder paints in a school art room.

Unexpectedly, the taverna has a menu, some of it in English. The list of main dishes is worth recording:

Local goat cooked with oil
Local goat with spaghetti
Local goat in the oven
Goat with tomato sauce
Goat tomato soup
Local rabbit with spaghetti
Fried rabbit
Local chicken with rice
Local goat with rice

No one else is here; harmless Greek music on the radio; a mural of a stylised sun with a red spiral in the middle, blue background, white border, something written in Greek, simply but beautifully done.

Pieter's work perhaps? Also a painted sign saying: 'Heureux qui comme Ulysse a fait de beaux voyages… Charles Baudelaire'.

'Pieter?' I say to the woman who runs the taverna and miming the act of painting in a far from convincing manner. 'Ah Pieter!' she says, but does she really understand?

Communication is limited, but she recognises the word 'food', showing me two pots with goat-like things inside. She also says 'Fava' which ought to be beans – the kitchen smells of fasoulia – and 'Salata', but I am a bit Greek salata'd out. I say: 'Fava' but she looks dubious. We shall see. Perhaps she is used to Greek appetites, where everybody eats twice as much as they should, which explains the shape of most Greeks over thirty – and much else.

Bread arrives, proper dark brown bread, the best I have eaten on the island since dining with the Russians in October. By a long way.

The fava turns out to be a mashed bean salad, a very rustic hummous with lots of olive oil, chopped raw onion and dried chilli. Enough for me, just right on an oval metal dish.

Back at the cafe in Agios Ioannis, I find I could have got all the news I'd been looking for had I only asked, but it is mostly bad news. The Russians have left the island, dispirited by the persistent insularity of the islanders and the hostility of church and state. Their temple was never built; the photograph I saw on the internet was just a mock up, and the row was much bigger than I could have guessed, the government threatening to deport them and the local archbishop even promising to have the entire population of the island thrown in prison if the building went ahead. Igor and Olga are now in Venezuela where the community has another of its mysterious bases. Arkady from Chernobyl is in Japan counselling survivors of their disaster.

While I have been away I have found a few more pieces for the jigsaw, and now I may never know where they fit, if at all. As well as juniper oil, the ancient Egyptians may have used a special kind of white clay in their embalming process; might it too have come from the island? Possibly the mysterious hebenus. Elsewhere, I read that white bentonite clay is sometimes used in the treatment of uranium poisoning. (I think it's eaten and it absorbs the toxins – the explorer

Colonel Fawcett came across remote villages in Amazonia where the population suffered a craving to eat mud as a result of some strange medical condition.) And the reason why Gurdjieff was in Sfakia when someone tried to assassinate him was that he was on the trail of the 'Imastun Brotherhood', survivors of the Gilgamesh flood, a secret organisation (so secret that no one other than Gurdjieff appears to have heard of it – backwards it reads 'Nuts am I') with cells around the world and a centre on a lost Greek island called 'Haninn'. He claims they were able to communicate with each other using telepathy: 'pythonesses' [not really anything to do with snakes, except in Delphi, but a general term for mediums; the name probably sharing a common stem with Pythagoras] received messages in trance, writing them down in a script that changed direction depending on where the information came from – left to right from the north, right to left from the south, top to bottom from the east and bottom to top from the west (mostly from Atlantis).

Pieter is in Paleochora with a broken shoulder, having crashed his bike, the inevitable accident on the familiar journey. 'What about Panos?' I ask.

'He's over there.'

'No he isn't.'

I have seen the man she is pointing at, several times before, something of a burnt-out case mumbling to himself in the corner. He hasn't even merited a mention in my notebook, not even 'he looks the way I sometimes feel' or 'all romantics end this way'. But I have noticed, although never recorded, that dogs love him – they trust him; he has something they recognise; every dog that passes by comes over to pay its respects – but it didn't seem relevant. Important things rarely seem relevant at the time.

Very few people are loved by dogs they don't own, only a select number. Who else? The prophet Elijah. Geoffrey Firmin in Under the Volcano, perhaps. Picasso liked to think he was. What other qualities do they share?

But it is Panos. And I don't know why I didn't recognise him. I would hate it if he thought I had been ignoring him.

He says he has seen me in the bar and has been meaning to come and speak, but things are difficult: His girlfriend, has left him; his drinking has got out of control; he has had a breakdown and stopped taking his medication; two days ago, he had a seizure while swimming and was found just in time lying face down in the water. He talks indistinctly, having bitten his tongue in the seizure. He doesn't want to leave the island and go to a hospital where he knows no one. He wants to stay here with his friends.

He begins to recite a poem or the lyrics of an old song, faltering at first, eventually with ease and there is something of the old Panos about him.

'Who wrote that?' I ask.

He looks at me with mock indignation. 'Do I need to give you two clues?'

'Tom Waits.'

Later Panos says: 'Whatever happened to Freedom? I use to go there so often in the sixties.'

'They fucked it up; they always do,' the words sounding oddly reassuring.

Chapter 37

2011

My new neighbours are a party of Greek women from the University of Heraklion and, for a week, this end of the beach is miraculously improved by their presence: tall, slender, loose limbed, long legged, excited to be here and full of a seemingly boundless energy that is almost infectious.

Youth should not be confused with beauty (few women under thirty can really be called beautiful, or so it seems to me now, although I probably thought differently when I was twenty-five), but there is a particular kind of elegance – or a fluency of movement – only seen in women of a certain age, between seventeen and twenty-two perhaps, and then rarely. The actress Jane Birkin had it briefly, also Charlotte Rampling. Sometimes it just depends on the extravagant way they swing their arms when walking.

Youth, of course, has its downsides and is probably best enjoyed at one step removed. The young suffer from insecurity, doubt and fear of failure even more than the old but it doesn't show on their faces or in their posture.

Almost all of it is an illusion; only the vitality is real. Life is an india-rubber ball dropped onto a hard surface, each time never quite bouncing back to its original height. And when young it is enough to have talent but no achievement.

I watch one of them, the most assured of all, Arrie reading architecture, long sandy hair, as she stands at the water's edge, alone and still, gazing out to sea, and I realise that James Joyce has been here before me. In A Portrait of the Artist, she seemed magically changed into the likeness of a strange and beautiful sea-bird, her long slender legs as delicate as a crane's. 'Heavenly God! cried Stephen's soul in an outburst of profane joy.' (Was the encounter a metaphor for Stephen Daedalus discovering his vocation as an artist? It always seemed to me, at least, to be one of the crucial moments of the book, but an abridged version I once read left it out entirely.)

In the cafe, Panos too is entranced, miraculously transformed, almost his old self again. He is in love; and Bob Marley is singing 'Every Little Thing Gonna Be Alright' in his honour.

Panos says: 'She is twenty-two and beautiful. I am a toothless old goat. That can't be bad.' (All young women love Panos.)

He is writing sub-Bukowski poetry on scraps of paper, dedicated to his latest love, full of promising ideas that with a bit of application – and not that much – might amount to something, but never will.

'How do you spell 'branches'?'

'With a 'ch' in the middle,' I say.

'What a bloody stupid language.'

And all manner of little things are going to be all right.

Very late one night I lie on the cold sand by the juniper, a time of night or place when the unknown becomes familiar and the familiar adopts a certain strangeness, a small cloud in the shape of a Dickensian night shirt floating ridiculously heavy in an otherwise clear night sky above us, while the moon is bright. Arrie puts down her guitar (improvised, lyrical, seriously accomplished, a very visual kind of music engendering elaborate, elegant, fractal patterns when I shut my eyes); she puts her face, very blue in the pale moonlight, close to mine – she smells subliminally of patchouli and tea tree oil; her gaze questioning, challenging, coolly assertive, a little like Leonardo da Vinci's Ginevra de' Benci (or possibly Titian's Venus of Urbino; the expression is very similar) – and she recites in faultless English with no trace of her usual accent some lines of poetry I cannot quite put a name to.

Her face against the sky is unusually distinct, as though emitting a faint radiance of its own. (Vladimir Nabokov has also been here before me.) She waits a few seconds for my response, but when it doesn't come she says: 'Louis MacNeice' and turns away. Very like Ginevra de' Benci.

Next morning, I cannot remember what the words were and am even further from knowing where they came from. The Island? Lines from an Unborn Child, perhaps? Were they important? Was it a private moment just for the two of us? A secret confided but not understood? A test failed? Was there a question I failed to ask, like Sir Bors at the grail castle?

Or perhaps I had imagined the whole thing; it was that time of night.

Chapter 38

2011

June drifts into July and beyond and the island changes. Friends leave, strangers arrive: people with dogs, cars, expensive tents they don't know how to put up, wooden bats and balls they play with all too proficiently, women wearing expensive bikinis, electronic music, more and more litter. Longer-term residents retreat to more distant beaches like latter-day Neanderthals; others go home.

The departure of friends is always odd, an intrusion of the outside world. Waiting for the ferry (usually problemo), waiting for the bus (always problemo), a reminder of past, worse times, intimations of future, worse times. Usually on the island there are no queues, no waiting, nothing to give you an awareness of time passing, beyond the daily round; when you want to swim or eat or go for a walk or go to bed you do so.

Goodbye Apostolis and Sevastine, Imogen, Rodrigo the guitarist, Peter and Agape with the beautiful eyes. See you next year, I say. But I know I won't. You never come back to the same island twice: you will not be the same people, prematurely aged by responsibilities and obligations, weighed down by possessions, tied by debts. You spend but an hour or two and make your way, and once departed may return no more. Time moves in mysterious ways with unpredictable currents, eddies and backwaters, but eventually, inevitably, it takes you away. You will never forget your week or two on the island but never imagine it could have been yours forever.

You will be very different people who disembark at Karave if you ever do again, but we who remain shall not grow old as you who are leaving grow old. Like Munchhausen and the Melmoth, dragons live for ever but not so girls and boys. We are moving to a different metre; a day here is a week or a month or a year in the world across the water.

And then one day, at first sight no different from any other, it is I who has to go. The angel with his darker draught draws up. And softly through the silence tolls the bell. Hurry up please it's time.

After profuse farewells, genuinely friendly, from Costas and all at the taverna, I set off to the harbour, looking for a lift (as expected, none to be seen). I walk all the way to the Korfos turn before the first car comes, and it stops as I knew it would. Sophia is at the wheel, and it seems the most natural thing in the world for me to be walking along the road and for her to stop; she always gives the impression of being one step ahead of you.

I have allowed three days to get from the island to the airport, which you may think is cutting it a bit fine, but when I get to the harbour I find a choice of three ferries waiting for me. One of them, which I haven't seen before, is supposedly running day trips from Plakias, arriving at midday and leaving at four, which is nowhere near enough time to go anywhere worth seeing. Today they have only one passenger; the crew are lounging in the taverna awaiting his return. Do people who work on the sea have a peculiar-distinctive way of sitting when ashore, where fishermen lounge at noon, a semi-recumbent stationary equivalent of the rolling gait when walking on a moving deck? Perhaps in August they will have more passengers; possibly not. I doubt if it will be here next year.

The 'Express' is also waiting, looking new and sleek, but no one, least of all the crew, knows when it is leaving or where it is going. Fortunately the Neptune is also there, leaving for Sougia sometime soon after lunch.

For once the bus is there too, but not the bus driver. Apparently, there has been an administrative misunderstanding with the bus company which is based in Athens and does not understand the ways of the island. He has been putting the fare money into one account and they felt it should be put into another, namely their own. (This may, of course, just be a story put about by other islanders; nothing anyone says should be taken at face value.)

As I go to sit down outside Anastasia's taverna, I somehow fail to recognise her husband sitting in the corner. This is bad, very bad. [Did I fail to see her son as well?]

As I sit on the drumming ferry, I suddenly wonder if I will ever come here again. Will I be able to find my way back through the labyrinth? I walk to the stern and stare at the receding outline of the island, making a conscious effort to remember the moment, and just for a second I am aware of myself feeling like the man in the Madox Brown painting.

This morning I found Dr Iorgos sitting with his feet in the sea and I shared my thoughts about time here moving at a different pace.

'I do not know if you are familiar with the work of the American folk-rock band The Eagles?' he said. 'They sang a song called Hotel California. It is like that here. I think this place is paradise.'

Chapter 39

2012

I have found a place for myself in the old cathedral city, somewhere to sit and write undisturbed. It is a table at the end, round the corner and out of the way in the beer garden of one of the older pubs, a cobbled yard on different levels with old walls (medieval stone topped with Tudor brick) heavily buttressed in more recent times against their ruin. The beer is the better kind of craftsman-made English bitter, although the pub is not a place I would want to sit inside even in winter. Too claustrophobic, too English. During the day it is frequented for the most part by old men who stop their conversations and stare when I walk in. (Later, they become more friendly, like the regulars on Lavrakas beach. One or two I become fond of. I shall miss them.) At night, not that I go there then, it is the usual riot as testified by the notices on the walls (fly-blown and disregarded), forlornly warning customers to leave more quietly otherwise the pub will lose its licence.

Service is slow whenever I visit, and often non-existent: I can stand at the bar for minutes without anyone appearing on the other side. Sometimes, eventually, I am served by a tall woman with sharply distinctive features and long purple hair. She usually wears an ankle-length black skirt, a basque and a low-cut top displaying impressively large tattooed breasts, heavily buttressed.

I once wrote a short story about someone who looked a bit like her, but the magazine I wrote it for closed or changed direction just as I was about to send it off to them, so I never did. I was rather pleased with the story, but there is no way of telling if it was any good. A competent writer can produce a well-crafted piece of work along conventional lines and be reasonably confident that it will be acceptable to most readers and editors, but once you set off beyond your comfort zone you are in uncharted territory; you have passed out of the known world and are quite possibly on your own, or with only the Great McGonagall and the artist in Balzac's Le Chef d'Oeuvre Inconnu for company (like leading a cavalry charge and not knowing until you reach the enemy line whether anyone is following you). When people say they like something I've written there is always the possibility that it is all just an elaborate practical joke. I never know when to let the dog off the lead, when to keep it muzzled and when the most sensible option is to take it out the back and shoot it.

Around the same time I wrote a story about a spoon, 'The Teaspoon from the Bungalow Cafe', and I sent it to The Oldie and then to The Idler, but both sent it back unimpressed. I have become incapable of following a brief or writing to length, always feeling compelled to go a little further or more sideways than is sensible, almost as a deliberate provocation like Beatrix Potter's Squirrel Nutkin or Peter Rabbit, an incitement to the editor to reject it. 'I don't think the teaspoon quite stands up,' said the kind commissioning editor at the Oldie. I occasionally look at the story and wonder why no one else likes it as much as I do, or, more often, why it is I cannot see its faults. [Whimsicality and offensiveness is rarely a winning combination.]

The woman behind the bar looks at me severely, waiting impatiently for me to hand over the money for my pint. I hope she doesn't think I was staring at her breasts, although it is hard not to do so, particularly when thinking of other things (your eyes get drawn to them unintentionally; they follow you around the room).

I once saw someone like her many years ago, and there cannot be many people who look like that. One morning I had hitch-hiked back to London after an all-night party and walking through central London I had three very odd experiences in the space of half an hour. At the Lex garage in Monmouth Street in Covent Garden [now demolished and I would have difficulty identifying its exact location] I saw an old friend (Bob Cooper who worked at the British Museum) filling up with petrol, but, when I went up to him and said: 'I didn't know you drove a Light Fifteen', he replied: 'I think you've mistaken me for someone else'. The expression on his face was exactly like Bob's would have been in similar circumstances: at that moment, he probably looked more like Bob than Bob had ever done, but he denied all previous acquaintance.

(Whatever happened to Bob Cooper? He was allowed to drift away like most of my friends. One of those good lunchtime friendships in the Museum Tavern, an hour or two a day over two or three years, and once departed may return no more; Bob Cooper, Ivor Solomon [who maybe became an English literature academic at the University of East Anglia?], June Macready who kissed me goodbye before I left for India – when I eventually came back everything had changed, and I never saw them again, except possibly Bob on that single occasion. Perhaps, one day I will meet them all walking along the beach at Agios Ioannis.)

I would have questioned Bob, or pseudo-Bob, further but I was distracted by the dark grey flashes of lightning flickering from the overcast sky and converging on the top of a nearby building which appeared to be somehow harvesting the energy, a place of significant but not entirely desirable occult power; I went in search of it, curious that anything so blatant could have been operating in the middle of London without anyone noticing, and found it was Freemasons Hall – not, after all, as most people might assume, a largely defunct social club for businessmen with a few silly rituals thrown in for old times' sake.

Then at the beginning of Tottenham Court Road I saw, again unnoticed by anyone else, an eight-foot-tall woman with purple hair and a severe expression; she was floating, head and shoulders above the crowd, round the corner of Charing Cross Road and Oxford Street: she could (almost) have been the same person (but a little taller).

Out in the garden of the cathedral city pub, when the battery of my laptop has run down (annoyingly quickly), I open my new paperback copy of The Rings of Saturn and stare at the first page: 'In April 1992, when the dog days were drawing to an end...' It is not the words I am looking at; I have read them before and will again in other circumstances: it is the page itself that interests me. There was once a time when I sometimes designed things like that for a living and gave serious thought to how they were put together; it was a part of my life I rarely think about now, a door that has closed, no longer worth reopening, and I am shocked by how quickly knowledge disappears when it stops being of immediate use. I can no longer identify the typeface – perhaps one of the twentieth-century Garamonds like Sabon, but that is just a guess; I would have known once without thinking, but it doesn't matter now. It works successfully enough as a text face but less well as a two-line drop cap (or so it seems, although the self-imposed rules I once worked by may well have been false), and the left and right margins are tighter than I would have chosen; but the unusual amount of space between the words and the lines and above and below the block of text is oddly hypnotic, the whiteness resembling a thick mist drifting in from the sea, the spaces around and in between becoming almost as important as the words.

The tightness of the margins suddenly brings me up short, reawakening a forgotten memory, probably best forgotten, of a book I once designed in odd circumstances. I had been rung one morning by a stranger with an American accent, name long ago forgotten, who said he was looking for a designer and I had been recommended by a writer in Los Angeles whose name I didn't recognise. We arranged to meet at a restaurant in Wapping in East London, but instead of going inside for a meal or a drink we sat in the car park while he explained what the job entailed: a valuable cache of Beatles photographs had come into his possession (he didn't explain how) and although he had no publishing experience he wanted to turn them into a book himself rather than hand them over to a proper publisher (he didn't say why); he would pay cash, half in advance, the rest on completion. It was a difficult job to put a price on, with nothing much to go on, but the figure agreed turned out to be more than adequate (for once). So many things can go wrong in jobs like that, but amazingly nothing did, or didn't appear to. Everything turned up on time, the copy from the writer in Los Angeles who somehow had heard of me was all to the agreed length; I was able to do what I wanted with the typefaces and page design (based on the proportions of a medieval illuminated manuscript, name forgotten, with reference to the square root of minus two, not than anyone else would ever notice or care, a private joke shared only by me and myself). I handed over the disk in the same car park, received an envelope of used £50 notes in exchange and never heard from the man again or ever saw a copy of the book, even on Amazon.

A year or so later I remembered with a sudden flinch that at our first meeting he had said that the book would be ring-bound which meant that the generous inside margin that I had originally planned would have been hopelessly inadequate. He might even have had to pulp the whole print run and start again.

It would be a mistake to infer from this story, or from any of the others in this book, that my working career was particularly interesting, eventful or in any memorable way distinguished. I would have been lucky to have found a job that fitted my somewhat unusual mix of talents (and otherwise), so I never really looked for one. Career structures are not designed for people who are 'different'; jobs on the lowest rung have tasks that are easy for 'normal' people, whose minds run on tracks, but are more difficult for 'different' people. The jobs that 'normal' people struggle with but 'different' people find easy are much higher up the ladder, but to get there you have to have excelled at the lower levels. 'Different' people make up a very high percentage of 'geniuses', but most of us are destined for a life of failure. Homo Sapiens was nowhere near as clever as Neanderthal but better at networking, at hunting in packs; Neanderthal was the cat that walked by himself. Modern people are said to have about five per cent of Neanderthal genes. Perhaps some of us have more.

When broke, I usually took the first work that came along and stuck at it for a few months until I had saved enough money to live for a while without the daily drudgery. (And when I left university, most permanent jobs offered only three weeks holiday a year; it wasn't an option for anyone who wanted an adventurous life.)

Mostly, when in England, I lived cheaply in South London squats, turning fifty before I took my first 'proper' job, a bit late for a career by most standards, and then only because of financial necessity (it wasn't a good idea, as I knew it wouldn't be; after a few years my health broke down, pretty much for good). Mine was no worse a way to live a life than most and certainly better than many, but it is an option no longer available, not one my children can choose – the pressure to conform and the penalties for transgressing or breaking ranks are now too great.

Returning to The Rings of Saturn, I notice that the mist-like effect of the white space is increased by the cheap matt paper which suffers from 'show-through' so that the text and photograph on the following page are visible if indistinct, like objects looming out of a mist. The picture, when you turn the page, is of a somewhat opaque window, ostensibly taken from Sebald's hospital bed, the glass reinforced by a wire mesh in a diamond pattern.

It is not the kind of photograph I often wanted to take in the years when I was interested in photography although the rules I worked by may well have been false. The photographs I took were 'unquestionably odd' but often admired, finding patterns and connections not immediately obvious to other people, the kind of photographs that would cause anyone flicking through a magazine to stop, go back and wonder what it was doing there; definitely 'clever' but now when I see them my first thought is: 'Yes, but so what?' I now suspect photography is best used as a simple record of interesting things. [Perhaps the same is true of writing?] But I once did something similar to Sebald's photographs – lying on my bed in a shed on the roof of one of the rougher flop houses in Old Delhi (four rupees a night) and deciding for no particular reason to take a photograph every minute or so until the film ran out, not moving the camera at all but shooting whatever or nothing was happening in the room directly in front of my bed and through the open doorway on the flat roof outside, just to capture the moment, as it were; as it was, nothing happened, nothing at all, and it wouldn't have mattered if it had because the difference between light and dark inside and out was far too great to produce a printable negative, as I should have known.

The show-through of the paper in The Rings of Saturn makes the photograph of the window a (probably unintentional) gateway between the you that is reading the first page and the you that will later read the next, like the beginning of an oxbow. Is this relevant to my daughter's dissertation on the artistic interpretation of time? [Probably not.]

Chapter 40

2012

Pictures on the wall in the pub gents lavatory celebrate the city's more distinguished sons, but it is not an impressive list. For some reason the composer is missing; Watkins is there understandably enough although his citation dwells less on ley lines than on his supposed invention of the photographic light meter. He was born, the poster tells me, in the Imperial Hotel in Widemarsh Street which has since gone badly downmarket: now on Thursday nights it offers as an attraction to visitors half-price 'Snakebite', a fifty-fifty mixture of bitter and cider, a drink with such a bad reputation that most pubs refuse to serve it let alone advertise it.

A thin-lipped bare-knuckle prizefighter called Tom Spring (real name Tom Winter, more appropriate) glowers from his poster above the next stall; I have known several professional boxers and without exception they were decent, gentle people, far gentler than they should have been, an interesting paradox that others have commented on before (that is also true of the few murderers I have known, and also terrorists like the beekeeper on the island); Spring, however, is clearly an exception – by the look of him he is a thoroughly nasty piece of work (with, if the contemporary portrait on the poster is to be believed, very small feet and no testicles). His last fight was against an Irishman called Langan who was beaten senseless in seventy-six rounds; 'a long and dreadful fight,' the poster adds a little unnecessarily. Spring's fists were so damaged by the pounding he inflicted that he was incapable of fighting again; later he became the landlord of the Booth Hall pub down the road (now the 'Home of the £2 Lunch') – I cannot imagine anyone worse as a landlord – but 'to celebrate Tom Spring's achievements', whatever they might have been, the Wye Valley Brewery has produced a beer in his honour called White Knuckle.

A self-portrait by a painter called Brian Hatton peers down from above the third stall, a nice enough chap as far as one can tell, killed in 1916 alongside my grandfather, along with all the others. 'Had he lived,' the poster says, 'he might have become one of Britain's greatest artists', but on the evidence of the pictures in the poster this opinion is hopelessly optimistic. Nonetheless, 'The Wye Valley Brewery is happy to honour his name in its beer "Artist's Revival"'.

I will be surprised if they ever include me in this pantheon of local heroes even though the empty space above the fourth urinal, albeit Duchamp-esque, hardly compares in terms of prestige with, say, the empty fourth plinth in Trafalgar Square. Perhaps the Wye Valley Brewery will one day be pleased to honour my name or celebrate my achievements in its beer 'Miserable Git', but that is most unlikely.

Chapter 41

2012

I sometimes wonder if Sebald was familiar with the MR James short story Whistle and I'll Come to You, My Lad; James was hardly a major writer of fiction and unlikely to be of much interest to distinguished German academics, even those with eclectic interests, but it contains one of the scariest episodes in twentieth-century English literature and it takes place unforgettably somewhere along the stretch of coast covered by Sebald in The Rings of Saturn [Not quite; he abruptly veers off inland about three hundred yards before]; his and James's protagonists will have clambered over the same groynes, presumably both authors too.

Late one evening after his round of golf, James's Parkins, a Cambridge professor of 'ontography', stops to investigate the ruins of a nearby templar presbytery, which is never a good idea in James stories. There he unearths an old metal object among the rubble, and examining it later in his hotel room he finds it to be a whistle bearing the legend

Fla

Fur   Bis

Fle

and on the other side, bracketed by two swastikas, 'Quis est iste qui venit'.

When blown, the noise is disappointingly thin, almost like a dog whistle, but a sudden gust of wind seems to come in answer to his call. Later, he sees a wanderer on the shore looking up at his room. Like many writers, perhaps more now than then [perhaps not], James uses the sea as a metaphor for the human subconscious, particularly as the realm of monsters, slowly but insistently encroaching: 'Whatever may have been the original distance between the Globe Inn and the sea, not more than sixty yards now separated them.'

In my latter days as a travel journalist I discovered by chance that the 'Globe Inn' at 'Burnstow' where Parkins was supposed to have stayed was not a complete fiction but an actual place (with just a different name), somewhere that has seen better days and definitely not on the tourist map; it might have made a good story. (The 'Globe' has diminished, like many, into a downmarket pub with a few rooms. The original wooden hotel burnt down between the wars leaving only the brick extension where Parkins had stayed; a further addition in the 1960s of a single-storey glass extension now offers panoramic views of what has become a container port but adds little to the architectural interest. In Parkins' time, the Globe had chambermaids in uniform, and the conversation in the dining room between the secretary of a London gentleman's club and the vicar, 'an estimable man with inclinations towards a picturesque ritual, which he gallantly kept down as far as he could', would now probably be drowned by the noise of the televised football; and neither of them would have enjoyed or willingly participated in the advertised Wednesday night karaoke sessions.)

But I never went, partly due to failing health and other complications, and partly because I was trying and failing to trace another James short story also set in a Suffolk seaside hotel, quite possibly the same one. I had read it in a nineteen-twenties anthology of ghost stories (Machen, Le Fanu and many other worse writers now forgotten) but the spine broke, the book fell apart and I binned it not thinking I would ever need it again. Amazingly, despite my best efforts, I found that the story has also disappeared, as though it had never existed, much like the mysterious Room Thirteen in the other James hotel story, a suitably Jamesian phenomenon but very inconvenient in terms of my article.

Eventually the fiction of what I might have experienced had I gone there materialised to such an extent that no space was left for the actuality of what I might have encountered. ('"Are you down here on..."' said the imposing landlady of striking appearance, but she couldn't think of the right word, or indeed any word. When booking, I had specifically asked for the first-floor front room with the big bay window – a "family" room as she had made a point of telling me – but I had arrived on my own. When Professor Parkins stayed here over a century ago, he had been disconcerted to find that this was the only one available – for reasons not explained, he was uncomfortable with the idea of sleeping in a room with an empty bed beside him. I, on the other hand, was insisting on it even though other, more suitable and cheaper rooms were available, which puzzled the landlady even more. Neither she, nor anyone else perhaps, is aware that possibly the scariest episode in twentieth-century English literature took place under her roof,' etc. etc. It pretty much writes itself.)

As Parkins lies in bed, a vivid waking dream appears uninvited whenever he shuts his eyes: someone at the end of his strength is running along the beach clambering with increasing difficulty over the groynes, eventually collapsing terrified and exhausted on the shingle below Parkins' window. In the distance, a figure emerges from the darkness dressed in pale, fluttering drapery. 'There was something about its motion which made Parkins very unwilling to see it at close quarters,' is how James puts it. 'It would stop, raise arms, bow itself toward the sand, then run stooping across the beach to the water-edge and back again; and then, rising upright, once more continue its course forward at a speed that was startling and terrifying. The moment came when the pursuer was hovering about from left to right only a few yards beyond the groyne where the runner lay in hiding. After two or three ineffectual castings hither and thither it came to a stop, stood upright, with arms raised high, and then darted straight forward towards the groyne.' Occasionally when alone at the far side of twilight on Agios Ioannis beach I have felt tempted to perform the same ritual, but I never have [and probably won't do so now].

Parkins keeps his candle burning for the rest of the night.

Next day, he experiences a series of disturbing events. The other bed looks as though someone had been sleeping in it: 'Why, all the things was crumpled and throwed about all ways, if you'll excuse me, sir,' says the maid. An equally implausible urchin is terrified by something he sees 'wiving' at him from the professor's window. That night, Parkins is woken by the said something approaching from the other bed with an 'intensely horrible face of crumbled linen', and then unfortunately it all gets rather nasty, although James has the decency not to elaborate, and at the end, like Beatrix Potter, he pretends it all wasn't really very bad.

James makes an interesting contrast with the American writer of horror stories HP Lovecraft, particularly in their use of language – Lovecraft will have exhausted all the extreme adjectives in his repertoire and be resorting to inventing new ones in the time it takes James to apologise for suggesting that the 'thing' in question might not be entirely dead or entirely alive. But both have a hallmark of authenticity, essential for an effective ghost story: with Lovecraft, you suspect that anyone with so little natural aptitude for writing must have had something important to say otherwise he would not be attempting anything so unsuited to his abilities; James, on the other hand, clearly knew his demonology, both biblical and Templar, and may have dabbled a little too deeply, discovering something genuinely nasty in the library and he could never resist going back time and again to see if it was still there, and hadn't changed much since he last inspected it. (Something is happening but you don't know what it is, do you MR James? Or perhaps you do, all too well.) And although he never went there, Lovecraft's psychological landscape had its origins in the Suffolk coast with its decaying towns and encroaching sea.

Like many schoolmasters of his time (and later), James enjoyed frightening small boys in the dark, and the bare bones of Whistle and I'll Come to You, My Lad appear to the modern reader to reveal an underlying theme of repressed homosexuality which might not have been obvious years ago. James would have been horrified had anyone suspected; the tide has gone out uncovering more that he would have liked. With its themes of the Suffolk coast, sexual unothodoxy and the presence of inexplicable evil, it is surprising that Benjamin Britten never based an opera on the story. (You may have noticed that I have rightly restrained myself from finding a cheap pun on the word groyne.)

Most of James's work has not aged well. Characterisation and dialogue are no longer believable, particularly that of the 'lower orders': James was incapable of understanding or respecting anyone who could not conjugate a Latin verb correctly. The humour is so dry that it long ago crumbled into dust. But many of his stories are still genuinely scary. And I particularly like Karswell, the villain in Casting the Runes, who persisted in sending unpublishable articles to leading academic and literary journals and, when rejected, wreaking a terrible but no doubt deeply satisfying revenge on their editors.

Chapter 42

2012

I am killing time in the cathedral, a very MR James-like activity, in the vague hope of learning a little more about Thomas Traherne, one of its longer-term residents, when it occurs to me that I ought to give the famous map a closer inspection on the unlikely offchance that it might have some relevance to my island – too much to hope that it has anything to say about Ogygia but the island might get a mention because of its somewhat tenuous association with St Paul.

A reproduction on sale in the bookshop shows Crete directly below the Holy Land (Jerusalem is the centrepoint of the circular map) and, offshore in the direction of Egypt, is a small oblong island with a faint, barely decipherable legend in gothic script; I can just about make out what, with a lot of wishful thinking, might be the name 'Calippso'. I show the picture to the shop manager for a second opinion; she thinks it looks more like 'Adippfo' but suggests I ask the exhibition curator who should know more; he doesn't, nor can either of us read the letters on the actual map with any certainty but he refers me to the definitive work on the subject by Scott D Western of City University New York; and Western's photograph of the 'Eastern Mediterranean' section of the map has the reference number 1031 above the island next to the gothic letters. Leafing through the back of the book I find note 1030 at the bottom of a page, turn it over and the first word I see is 'Calippso', a good moment – so it wasn't a dream after all. It cannot just have been a coincidence: coincidences rarely if ever happen precisely where and when you hope they will.

Western may have been briefly puzzled as to why Calypso's island should have been put next to Crete, but he sees no reason to disagree with Livy who identified it with a small island off Cape Colunna in Italy; he assumes it to be simply another example of the map's geographical inexactitude (Delphi is famously confused with Delos.). In his book The Cosmographia of Sebastian Munster, Matthew Adam McLean (of whom I know nothing else) says that compilers of medieval world maps were 'uninterested in fidelity to empirical knowledge of the world. Geographical features considered worthy of inclusion were mental rather than topographical landmarks.' That is also true of Homer (and of me too). Much of the Odyssey was based on older sources later lost, myths once specific to a particular place and drawing their power from them: but the places were not always where he said they were in the book.

In later Classical times, Ogygia was still occasionally associated with my island despite an absence of corroborating evidence, then not at all in the middle ages, or so it seemed. Perhaps the designer of the cathedral's map knew someone who had visited my island on his journey back from the crusades or a pilgrimage and stumbled on a secret shared only by a few.

Chapter 43

2012

I have seen a house for sale and would very much like to buy it, but I don't suppose we will. It is called Jerusalem Cottage, Durcotte Common, one of those beautiful, back end of nowhere places, real country not smart country (or, even worse, genteel country), rough at the edges, on the side of a hill surrounded by fields and woodland with occasional views across half the county.

It is still a place Dorothy Hartley's imaginary mercenary, my medieval alter ego, might have recognised. Bloody and concussed, a loser in a cause to which he had no commitment, he was found lying in a ditch by a camp follower in the aftermath of a disastrous battle; travelling at night, 'starving on stolen food', they made their way slowly upstream until they could find a place where they felt safe. They would have been in constant danger from gangs of the victorious army roaming the countryside undisciplined and exuberant in their enthusiasm for killing anyone they could (when the battle was still in doubt they were probably at the back). The modern hermit is fleeing from their direct descendants, searching for refuge above the tide mark of mediocrity and 'respectability', somewhere safe from the sick hurry and the dull-witted fire of claustrophobic ugliness and ferocious stupidity.

Jerusalem Cottage is nothing special, probably damp with low ceilings and inadequate insulation, but I can still almost afford to buy it and owe nothing to anyone. It is just about big enough with three bedrooms for whenever the children need a safe house, a still point in a turning world. A main road with one of the last effective bus services in England is only half a mile away down the hill but the lane passing the door is a no-through road, a cul-de-sac, an impasse, with a mohican of grass up the middle and it rarely sees more than five cars a day, although the local composer (minor in world terms but probably no worse for that) would have come here on his sit-up-and-beg boneshaker bicycle listening to the sound of the trees. The cottage has a garage, not a thing of beauty but useful for storing unwanted possessions, the things that no one can quite bring themselves to throw away, and space off the road for the car when we can no longer afford to tax it; the garden has a greenhouse, a shed, a vegetable patch, and a large, seriously ancient yew tree. The composer might have stopped here, pretending to admire the tree and claiming to his cycling companion that the sound of the wind in its branches was suggesting a possible opening theme for the third movement, but really just catching his breath. It will hardly have changed since then, a moment in its long lifespan. Had he come this way, my medieval mercenary would have seen it too, looking much as it does now.

Best of all, Jerusalem Cottage has a small, run-down orchard with a summerhouse at the end. The apple trees had been planted in straight lines on ridge and furrow, now with many gaps between them. I would reinforce the original grid pattern, replacing the missing trees with old cider apple varieties, damsons, quinces, mulberries and some improbable ornamental trees of appropriate size and shape, ones that could masquerade as any old apple until they come into flower and reveal themselves as something alien. Or maybe I might only plant native species or those that might have grown there in the thirteenth century (with maybe a few exotics that the hermit would have known in the Holy Land or on his way home), creating a haven from where all the vicissitudes of the last eight hundred years have been excluded. And I would grow wild roses over the hedges and through the less productive trees, plant bluebells in the furrows and daffodils on the ridges so that it begins to resemble a series of parallel tunnels (perfect circles with the branches of the trees overlapping overhead), and I would insulate the summerhouse, line it with bookshelves, put in a wood-burning stove and an occasional bed, and I could sit on the veranda under a turf or corrugated-metal roof and write about the small things that happen – the taste of our home-made bread, beer, cider and honey (such food as this poor farm and my slender patrimony provides) – or about the things that have always been here and will still be here after I've gone: the pattern of the leaves on the grass, or sunlight through the trees, or the sounds you hear in quiet places, nothing with clever subtext or layers of meaning, not for publication or 'posterity', and not for the sake of a ribboned coat or the selfish hope of a season's fame, but an end in itself, just for the moment. Perhaps it is enough to be at peace with the moment, with where we are now.